THE BOOK OF
THE TEN MASTERS

PURAN SINGH

SINGH BROS.
AMRITSAR

ISBN 81-7205-148-4

Reprint by Singh Bros.
May 1995

April 1998

Price : Rs. 60-00

Publishers :
SINGH BROTHERS, MAI SEWAN, AMRITSAR.
Typesetters :
K. G. Graphics, S.C.O. 98, City Centre, Amritsar.
Printers :
Printwell, 146, Industrial Focal Point, Amritsar.

INTRODUCTION

The history of human civilization took a new turn when the Sikh Gurus appeared on the scene of Medieval India. It was a time when people had no sense of the real meaning of life and were indulged in useless ritualistic pursuits. The Sikh movement served as a light-house for the people groping in the dark. The people converged around this light-house, listened the ambrosial sermons to their heart, and got imbued themselves in the Divine tremors. The Master showered on them the real 'gift of life' (*Jia dān*) and unified them with the Almighty God (*Har sio lain milāe*). They were then changed men and elevated to the stage of the ideal man i.e. *Gurmukh*. The Sikh history narrates many heart-rending stories of such elevated disciples.

Prof. Puran Singh (1881-1931 A.D.) was a genius of his times. Though he got his higher education in Chemistry and earned a good name in this field with new researches, he basically was a man of letters. He had a good habit of enjoying the company of spiritualists and sharing his spiritual experiences with others. For that he joined the other mystic folds too, but when he came in contact with the Saint-Sikh poet Bhai Vir Singh, he was infatuated by the Sikh mystic path. He treaded this path and shared his emotional feelings with others in the form of a number of books. His Punjabi and English mystic poetry touches the new heights of spiritual experiences in a powerful but simple language.

The historians' accounts of the Sikh Gurus narrate the political, social and other events exhaustively but they lack the spiritual horizon of the Great Masters. It was Puran

Singh, who touched this aspect in depth. Himself a mystic par-excellence, he narrates the stories in his own way. The flow of the narration is unparalleled. The reader absorbs himself with the first sentence and enjoys the Divine Masters' blessings to his heart.

When the world is by and large dissatisfied on account of inner spiritual hunger, we find that the mystic writings of Puran Singh serve as a soothing healer to the strife-torn humanity. Therefore, such writings must be published again and again so that a large number of people could take benefit from these. We are feeling an inner satisfaction when we find ourselves attached with this rare and marvellous writing. This is the feeling which we cherish for our esteemed readers by its publication.

—*Publishers*

CONTENTS

Foreword : Ernest Rhys   13-20

I—THE FIRST MASTER : GURU NANAK   21—47

The Child Nanak   21
The Boy Nanak   22
Nanak the Strange Youth   23
Nanak the World Teacher   24
Nanak and his Sister   26
Nanak and Duni Chand   27
Nanak and a Jeweller   28
Nanak at Eminabad   28
Nanak and the Tantrik Koda   28
Nanak and Sajjan Thug   29
Nanak and Vali Qandhari   29
Kamal and Brahamdas enter Discipleship   30
Nanak and a Poor Man   32
Nanak and the Leper   32
Nanak and God's House   33
Nanak and Two Cities   33
Nanak and the Fools   34
Nanak at Hardwar   34
Nanak at Kurukshetra   34
Nanak and Emperor Sikandar Lodi   35
Nanak at Jagannath   35
Arti (Hymn of Praise)   35
Nanak and Nur Shah of Assam   36
Nanak and the King of Sangladip   37
Nanak and Baber's Invasion of India   37
The Massacre of Saidpur   39

The Master and the Cohorts of Baber   41
Nanak and the Emperor Baber   41
Nanak and Mardana   42
Nanak and His Wheat Farms at Kartarpur   43
Nanak and Brother Lehna   44
The Saffron Anointings   45
Nanak and His Departure from This Planet   45

II—THE SECOND MASTER : ANGAD NANAK   48—57

Pilgrimage by the Old Nanak to the New   48
The Ecstasy of Love   48
Angad on the Roadside   49
The Playmates of Angad   52
Angad and the People   52
Moths Round the Lamp   52
Angad's Power   52
Angad and Emperor Humayun   53
The Three Temples of Angad   53
Angad and His Disciple Amardas   53
New Cities Spring   55
Samadhi of Love   55
The Disciple Crowned   56

III—THE THIRD MASTER : AMARDAS NANAK   57—65

The Poor Servant   57
The Master's Injunction against Caste   57
The Humour of Amardas   58
Bibi Bhani   58
The Choice of the Bridegroom   59
How the Fragrance Spread   59
Jetha   61
The Jealousy of the Aristocrats   61
The Master at Thaneshwar   62
Amardas and His People   62

Amardas and the Emperor Akbar 63
Amardas and Jetha 63
The Bridegroom Crowned 64

IV—THE FOURTH MASTER : RAMDAS NANAK 66—69

Ramdas and Baba Sri Chand 66
Ramdas and Amritsar 66
Ramdas and Arjun 97
The Disciple's Time of Exile 68
Songs of Arjun 68
The Son Crowned 69
The Poetry of Ramdas 69

V—THE FIFTH MASTER : ARJUN DEV NANAK 70—82

The Book of the Disciples 70
The Tarn Taran 70
Hari Mandir 71
The Sikh Epoch 72
The Composition of Guru Granth 72
Arjun Dev and His People 75
Arjun Dev as Husband and Father 76
Arjun Dev and His Brother Pirthi Chand 78
Arjun Dev and the Prince Khusro 79
Arjun Dev the Poet Prophet and People's King 81

VI—THE SIXTH MASTER : HAR GOBIND NANAK 83—94

The Affliction of the Soul of the People 83
The False King and The True King 85
Har Gobind's response to the Dhyanam of
    His Disciples 87
Har Gobind and Shah Jehan 89
The Master and His Disciples 91

VII—The Seventh Master : Har Rai Nanak   95—96

VIII—The Eighth Master : Har Krishan Nanak 97—98

IX—The Ninth Master : Tegh Bahadur Nanak   99—103

Tegh Bahadur and Amritsar   101
Birth of Gobind Rai   102
Bala Pritam, The Child-Beloved   103

X—The Tenth Master : Gobind Singh Nanak 109—136

Anandpur of the Tenth Master   109
Malin or The Gardener's Wife   110
Bhai Nandlal and Ghyassuddin at Anandpur 112
Gobind Singh in Disguise   113
Gobind Singh and Renunciation of the Sanyasi 114
The Ancestor of the Punjab Kalals   114
The Call of the Master   115
The Disciples Baptise the Master   118
Akali   119
Hansa Enters the Path of Discipleship   122
Padma, Daughter of the Rajah of Nahan   124
The Hill Rajahs, The Tools of the Moghal Empire 125
Said Khan Enters Discipleship   126
The Master Besieged   128
The Sweetness of Death   129
Two Pathans Help the Master   130
The Two Princes Betrayed   131
The Forty Martyrs   132
Love Gathering Again   133
The Mystic Fire   133
Abchal Nagar   134
The Word Crowned   135

XI—GURU NANAK : GLIMPSES OF HIS ART AND THOUGHT 137—152

Nanak and His Poetry   137
Japji   141
A Hymn of Nanak   143
Love   147
All is Well, if I am with Him   147
Karma   148
Woman   148
The Temple of Bread : Langar   149
Nanak gives New Meanings to Old Words,
    as did Buddha   151

XII—GURU GOBIND SINGH : SELECTIONS AND FREE
    TRANSLATION FROM THE DASAM GRANTHAM   153—159

  I. From Vachitar.Natak   153
  II. From Akal Ustat   153
  III. From Jap Sahib : The Hymn of Salutations 156
  IV. To His Disciples   157

"Sarv Rog Ka Aukhad Nam."   —*GURU GRANTH*
"His name is the cure of all distress."

"Music is His food, and the colours of life are His raiment."   —*NANAK*

Fellow-Traveller on the Path of life, stay awhile. Let me tell you a few things that we heard as Sikh children from our ancestors, and let me share with you the Song of Nanak, which is our only provision for the pilgrimage from this earth to that Heavenly Region where the Masters dwell in peace.

Gwalior, C.I.,   **PURAN SINGH**
May, 1920

FOREWORD

"It is the Master's gift—this life of inspiration. All the Gods exist in the Master—Shiva, Vishnu, Brahma; and the Vedas are in Him, and the Divine Song."

The Book of the Ten Masters is the record of the teachers of the Sikhs, who have handed on the mystic doctrine first taught by Guru Nanak in the sixteenth century. Nanak is "the unknown man who roams disguised on earth", who enters into the vacant house, the heart of his disciples, through whom the mystery of the divine in men is revealed. A poem of Puran Singh in an earlier volume[1] says, "Nanak is still with us, a Song, a Book, ...his voice still sings in our ears, his figure flits before us, his eyes meet ours, his feet we touch." He is part of the Changing Permanence of Things Eternal, which is one of the secret doctrines of the sacred Book of the Sikhs, the Guru Granth.

Nanak, the first Master, not only lives in his disciples; His spiritual self, his very presence, passed into the mind and body of the nine Masters who were his successors. "Him have I seen not once, but for ten generations." After him, Angad received the sacred message and became the apostle of his inspired faith in God. To Angad, succeeded Amar Das. "I saw Amar concealing the All-Father in a majestic form of man, the silver knot of hair on high, the white beard flowing down like a river of light, a tall ancient stern man of love and labour; for behold, Nanak is now become Amar Das." So the succession goes on and in the following pages the Western reader will be able to find the opening into that region of ecstasy which was sealed of Nanak and entered by his true disciples.

---

1. *The Sisters of the Spinning Wheel*, Dent & Sons, Ltd., 1921.

But while the line of the Gurus, of Saints and Masters of the Sikh religion, was maintained, there was a break in the tradition after the fourth, Ram Das. Already in his time a change had begun to affect the people. He it was, who founded the Golden Temple at Amritsar, and planned the bathing tank from whose waters that city takes its name, which means the divine essence of the true Ambrosia. Under the next Master, fifth in the line, Arjun, the tank and the temple were completed. That meant a new stage in the growth of the Sikhs : they were becoming a propertied people, acquiring a collective religious and social sense. The Golden Temple of Amritsar was a symbol of their new consciousness. They worked to complete it with such desperate devotion and unsparing energy, that "when Arjun saw the state of their bodies, he wept for pity." Another sign. It was on Arjun's initiative, that the bible of the Sikhs, the Guru Granth took form, and the orally preserved sayings, songs and other remains of the four previous Masters or Gurus were written down. But Arjun's fame, and the growing wealth of his people, excited the envy of the Emperor Jahangir. He was attacked too because of the heretical doctrines, detected by the orthodox, in the Granth Sahib. Arjun was not to be moved. He was of the seed of the martyrs, and his doom was inevitable. He was put to torture—fire and water and boiling cauldron—he bore all firmly. The last message he sent through the Sikhs to his son and successor, Har Gobind, was one that sounded ominously the change from peace to war : "Let him sit armed on his throne, and raise as best he can an army at his right hand !" That was in the year 1606 A.D., and the religion of the Sikhs went through a gradual metamorphosis in succeeding years, and their quietist faith became more and more militant.

So Har Gobind, in the Song of the Masters, appears in warrior guise. As his father had presaged, he and his fellow-Sikhs were to learn the truth of the fatal proverb— Wealth must wear a sword !" Under Har Gobind and his successors, the Sikhs still strengthened their commonalty. With Tegh Bahadur, ninth of the Gurus, we come to the advent of an overwhelming enemy, Aurangzeb who vowed he would convert all within his reach to Islamism. When Tegh Bahadur heard the cry of the Sikhs, imploring his aid against Aurangzeb, he sat so still, that his small son (who became the last of the Ten Gurus), grew uneasy and questioned him :

"Father, why art thou so silent ?"

"My son," he said, "thou art still a child, and cannot know how the very earth is grieved at the great oppression (by the Turks). Yet none is brave enough to give up his life, in order to free the earth from the burden of Islam."

"Oh, Father thou art brave and thou art generous. Who is worthier than thou to free the Sikhs from the sons of Islam ?"

Then Tegh Bahadur knew that this path was to be the same as Arjun's, and he gave himself up to Aurangzeb, and suffered martyrdom and a cruel death for his people's sake. His son, another Gobind—Gobind Singh—became the most warlike of all the Sikh leaders and Gurus. In the Song of the Masters, he as the tenth reincarnation of Nanak, appears in the form of the Ancient Huntsman, before whose arrows flies the Stag of Death.

"He wears the starry crest. He carries the Hawk on his thumb, and bears aloft the flags of the Kingship of Heaven."

"His pennon waves. His flags flutter on the walls of Heaven. The Angels cry aloud to him, 'Hail, Lord and Master.' "

"The Rider on the Blue Horse; the Wearer of the Blue Robe, he leads the Sikhs, the armies of the Heroes, to defend the sacred cause and the purpose of God on earth."

The end of Gobind Singh was in keeping with his warrior's aspect. His four sons, mere boys, were cruelly ordered to execution by Aurangzeb;[1] and died fearlessly.

---

1. Actually the two elder sons Ajit Singh and Jujhar Singh laid their lives in the battle of Chamkaur fighting against armies of Aurangzeb, while the younger ones Zorawar Singh and Fateh Singh were bricked alive by the Nawab of Sirhind.
                                              —*Publishers*

Their mother took her own life by suspending her breath when she found she could not save them or aid her husband. Again Gobind Singh, while still his wounds from the last battle he had fought were only half healed, took up a mighty bow to try his strength, and his blood burst out afresh. *Sic itur ad astra.* With his last breath he left the beloved book, *the Granth Sahib*, to his disciples.

That is one account of his end. The story told in the latter pages of this book is not so dramatic; but it is more mysterious. When the predestined day came, Gobind Singh sent for the sacred offering—simply a coconut and five pice—and laid them before the Holy Book, the *Granth Sahib*. "The Word is Master now," he said, "Let all bow before Saint Book, as my successor !" Thereupon, attired in his symbolic blue soldier's dress, he mounted his blue war-horse, as Marko of the Serbs did his horse Sarac, rode away and vanished behind the spiritual veil of the sensual world.

It is no wonder that the Sikhs look upon Gobind Singh as their deliverer, he, who by his sword became the true defender of their faith. For he had realized with Socrates, as we read in Plato's Republic, that a state or a city must have that courage which is a kind of safe-keeping—"the safe-keeping of that wisdom which teaches what things and what kind of things are to be feared." It was the sacred Idea of the Sikhs which was imperilled and which as Gobind Singh knew had to be saved and "to be preserved alike in pleasure and in pain, in fear and in desire, and never to be cast away."[1]

There is a transcendental touch in this record of an end, which was in reality a new beginning. Milton's familiar saying about the Book which is the precious life-blood of a master spirit, treasured up to a life beyond life, receives a new meaning by Gobind Singh's committal of the sacred office to the *Guru Granth*. The living Spirit of the Ten Masters or Gurus, passes finally into the pages of the ever-living inspired Book, the Testament of the Sikh faith, the

1. Bk. IV, 427

revelation of the divine Father to "the Child lost in the World-Fair," as Puran Singh has it. Its message was that of Coleridge :

All thoughts, all passions, all delights,
Whatever stirs this mortal frame
All are but ministers of Love,
And feed his sacred flame.

The conflict of the Sikhs with the powers of Islam, which reached its climax under the Tenth Master, Gobind Singh, was one based on a fundamental religious difference. In an interesting study of the two creeds, Puran Singh points out that like the ancient Vedism, out of whose scattered remains, Hinduism arose, Islamism was incompatible with the real and ideal doctrine of Nanak and the nine Masters who carried on his work. The religious faith of Islam was akin to Hinduism, in its dual worship of principles that are contrary to those of Nanak and of Buddha.

"Islam was, in fact, extremely dualistic in practical life. As the conqueror's religion., it lost its original beauty of universal good-will, implicit in the faith and sacred name of Allah. These two civilizations met in India, whence the religion of Buddha had already been driven out, only to suffocate the religious life of the people. The Hindu and Muslim cultures met, clashed and died, after giving brief life to Hindu Muslim art and thought : they never met in a living faith of the people; nor did they give any impetus towards true contemplation or right conduct. Both the Hindu and the Mussalman became slaves of selfishness, in their common contempt of the common people. Opposed to both these civilizations in the *Dhyanam*, the inspiration alike of Buddha and Nanak, which comes of art, not of philosophy. Both these teachers insist on the attainment of the unflickering flame of *Dhyanam*, of a life—calm, unruffled, supremely felicitous. In Buddhistic history, they carved the image of Buddha in stones, while in the Sikh history they aimed at chiselling the image of Guru Nanak in living statues of human bodies. This realization was higher than anything art alone can do, but human nature still craves artistic expression. There ought to have been a great renaissance of art and letters in the wake of Sikh culture; and a beginning was made by the Tenth Guru at Anandpur, which assumed the proportions of a great Sikh university. But the Sikh culture was thrown into the fire by the Muslim emperors.

"Neither Buddha nor Guru Nanak insists on a metaphysical philosophy of life. The work before man really is to transmute himself into very God. The *Dhyanam* of Buddha is the way, and there is no other way. In comparison with this civilization of art, joined to life and to religion, the Hindu and Mussalman philosophic systems divorced from life are dead or derelict.

"Indeed the monastic tendency of Hindu philosophy and Hindu life had by Nanak's time, well-nigh killed the spirit of religion in India. After many ages, the sense of religious vision had awakened in the mediaeval Bhaktas, under the leadership of the Hindu philosopher, Ramanuj. But he could not found his new religion of mysticism without torturing the Vedanta philosophy; this religious movement did little beyond producing a few Bhaktas who were something between monks and householders, rapt in their own metaphysical reverie. The only exception was Kabir, a weaver, a Muslim by birth, whom Ramanand won as his disciple more through the latter's enthusiasm than the former's choice. Kabir, by his inheritance of Muslim ideas, was well fitted to shock those followers of Hinduism whose ritual went by the name of religion. He cleared the air, and his name to-day is the only bright and living memory of the awakening led by Ramanuj and Ramanand. But neither Kabir nor Ramanand had that mastery over the laws of spiritual life that would have enabled them to create a new spirit in India. They were voices of reform, but lacking the original power at whose signal the graves would open and the dead arise from their sleep. Still we do see in their awakening the forerunner of the coming of the Master in the Punjab. The Master saw the darkness, and he rose to scatter the ghosts of night under Heaven's own Inspiration, and on the authority of his own, direct realization of the Truth."

From the crude and often confused reports of the life of Gobind Singh that have come to us, we discern the noble figure of a true leader, a soldier of God, who deliberately set out to storm the strongholds of superstition and tyranny; and we find that he did it with unfailing power, making everyone confess his soul to him, the Master. A word, a song, a smile from him, was enough to search the hearts of the people; and as the Master gave to them, so he took the Living Word from their lips. Such words as *Yama*, *Destiny*, *Nirvana*, *Yoga*, *Atma*, *Anhad*, *Brahman*, *Para-Brahman*, *Guru*, *Sadhu* and *Saint* are caught from the people as they used them, and these terms were given back to them with the inner illumination that came from the personal sanction of the Master. The Sikh people saw the meaning of everything : life, love, death and afterlife in Him. The language of Nanak cannot be interpreted by taking it in its literal or traditional meaning. The simple word, *Hukam*, is a whole song in *Japji*—suggestive of a law of the Creator's Mind, that we cannot, indeed, clearly express it in modern philosophic phraseology because the Master is dealing with the secret laws of life and not with the thought-products of his mind as does a mere philosopher. The word, *Suniye*, literally "hearing" is visibly a simple word; but the Guru devotes four complete songs in its praise. The highest meaning we can think of is "Inspiration." Such words again as "Rama", "Krishna", "Govinda", "Raghunath", "Vedas", "Vishnu", carry in them the devotional fervour of centuries. The sentence, "Rama is my Beloved", began to have a new significance to the people, when it was weighed with their own personal devotion to the Master.

"Now that I have taken refuge in Thee, I look to none beside.

They tell me there is the Purana and the Quran;
They tell me there are gods like Rama and Rahima;
But I know none but Thee !
They tell me there are a hundred other scriptures,
    Vedas, and Smritis, and many sacred books;
But I need nothing beyond Thy Word !
I have heard of all of them; but there is no close
    companion between them and me.
Now that I have taken refuge at Thy feet
I look to none beside."

The faith of the Sikhs, we learn by this book, is a living one, inspired and reinspired by Divine Idea and by the Living Word that passes current in the mouths of the people. To understand it the Western reader needs to enter with sympathy into the mind, childlike spirit and religious imagination of the followers of Nanak. That can be learnt from many episodes in these innocent pages, such as the stories of Gobind Singh as a merry boy or as a man who had not forgotten his boyhood, or the account of the humility, humour and good-humour of Amardas who, when he was kicked by the would-be Master, Datu, said, "Honoured Sir, my old bones are very hard. They must have hurt your precious foot ?" With that he rubbed Datu's feet in deep reverence.

As a revelation of the inner mind of the Orient, in its transparent truth and faith the book is unique. We need to throw aside our modern disbelief to get on terms with so child-like a spirit, with a temper of mind which was gentle to fearfulness, yet brave and fierce as the four young sons of Gobind Rai, or as the lion-heart of that Master himself.

Ernest Rhys

I
THE FIRST MASTER
GURU NANAK

THE CHILD NANAK

He came like a song of Heaven, and began singing as he felt the touch of the breeze and saw the blue expanse of sky.

He was a child of smiles, and his eyes were silent and wise; he loved quiet of soul. He loved joy and thought.

Whoever saw the child, or touched him accidentally, praised God. A thrill of unknown delight came to anyone who lifted the child, or played with him. But none knew whence came to him that gladness of soul.

Everyone saw that he was the child of Heaven; he was so beautiful, so mysteriously fair in colour and form, with a radiance that was new to earth. He cast a spell that none could escape. Rai Bular, the Moslem Governor of the place of his birth, loved him both as a child and as a boy; the Brahman teacher loved him; whoever came in contact with him was irresistibly drawn to him.

His sister Nanaki saw from his very infancy in him the light of God, and kept her discovery a profound secret. She was the very first inspired by Heaven to be his disciple. Rai Bular was the second; he had seen that gleam of soul in Nanak, which is seen only once in many centuries, and even then by the rarest chance. In his old age Rai Bular cried like a child for his saviour.

Nanak the child gave the signs of Nanak the Saint and

Guru at a very early age. He composed music, he talked of
God and life; his untutored mind was a marvel to everyone.

The Boy Nanak

He ate little, slept little, and shut himself in his own
thought for days and days; and no one could understand
him.

He was sent to the school, but he could not learn
anything. "Teach me," said he to his teachers, "only this one
large letter of life. Tell me of the Creator, and the wonder
of this Great World."

Thinking he might do as a trader, his father gave him
a few silver coins to set him up in that way of livelihood.
But no ! Having started out, he feasted the saints of God,
and returned empty-handed. Then he was sent to take the
cattle out to graze; he drove out the herds upon the green
sward, and left them free to graze by themselves as he sat
alone. The solitude of the Indian noon was good for him,
for then the whole creation taught him the language of the
gods. He heard the songs of the shade. Every blade of grass
intoned a hymn in his ears. His animals loved him, came
near him, touched him, looked at him; they knew nothing
of any man's ownership of meadows that, for them, all
appertained to God. The cows could make no difference
between "his" grass and "my" grass; so a clamour arose, and
they drove our Nanak and his cattle from the fields. He was
declared a failure as a cowherd; though he loved to sit alone
with stars, and to talk to animals when they were in
distress.

People anxious about his health brought a physician,
for to them Nanak's unworldliness appeared insane. When
the physician put his fingers on the pulse of Nanak, the
boy's voice, which had been silent for days, came thrilling
with a new and unsurpassed sweetness :

"They have called the physician to me !
The poor doctor feels my pulse !

What can a pulse disclose ?
The pang is in my heart !
Their life is a disease, and they seek nothing else.
The doctors come to cure, when there is no cure for the
    pain of death.
Oh, physician ! why touch my pulse when the pain is
    in my heart ? Go back ! go back whence you came !
None has a cure for the pang of love.
I pine for my Beloved :
Who gave the pain, will cure it.
Oh, poor physician, what can a pulse disclose ?
You have no cure for me."

When the family Brahman came to invest him with the
sacred thread, he spoke again, subduing all that heard :

"Oh, Brahman ! You have no sacred thread.
If you have,
Give me the forgiveness of the Creator,
Draw round me a sacred line that no desires dare cross,
Unfold the Divine in me,
Which then will be a sacred thread—
Never showing wear or break.
Fires shall not burn it, nor the storms destory !
Blessed of God, O Brahman, is the man such thread
    surrounds !
That is salvation."

NANAK THE STRANGE YOUTH

They married him, believing marriage and home-life
would bring him back to earth. And they asked him to set
out and earn a living for his wife. Nanak started to
Sultanpur, where his loving sister Nanaki lived. It was
thought that Jai Ram, Nanaki's husband, would get him
some employment. As he was setting out from Talwandi,
his native place, his wife came to him and said, "Pray, take
me, too, with you." "Dear lady," said he, "I go in search of
work; if I succeed, I will send for you."

Jai Ram got Nanak the position of officer-in-charge of the storehouse of Daulat Khan Lodi, Nawab of Sultanpur. Nanak loved to distribute the provisions; it is here that he began distributing himself also. None begged at Nanak's storehouse in vain, he lavished his goodness on every comer. It is said of him in a Punjabi proverb that God gave him His stores and then forgot all about them; key, lock, all were with Nanak.

It is here that he sang his famous song of one word. In Punjabi language, the word *Tera* means, both the arithmetical figure *thirteen* and the phrase *I am thine*. Once Nanak, weighing out wheat flour, counted the weighings—"one, two three"—till he reached the number thirteen; but at this he forgot all his counting and went on weighing and calling out : "*Tera ! Tera ! Tera ! Tera ! Tera ! Tera !......*" "Thine ! Thine ! Thine ! Thine ! Thine ! Thine !"

NANAK THE WORLD-TEACHER

He was lost in this flood of his own thought and wonder, a river that flowed out of him and at the same time engulfed him, so that he was looked on as one dead. What they saw of him was but as his garment cast upon the shore of life, while Nanak himself was swallowed by the Infinite. Truly, never did they see him again in the form in which they knew him so well. He came out and spoke as Guru Nanak the world-teacher, to the awe of everyone. Said he, "There is no Hindu, no Mussalman !"—a heresy so paralysing that they felt bound to suppose he had now lost every particle of sense. He could no longer take an interest in his work, and shortly afterwards left it altogether. He was not Nanak now, but Guru Nanak.

His father came to counsel him, but without effect. Of the many conversations that he had with his parents, on different occasions when he returned to his native place again and again from his travels abroad, we faithfully preserve the following few, without attempting chronological order :

Father : My son ! They say you do nothing, I am ashamed of you. Why not plough the fields if you can do nothing else ?

Nanak : I do something that others cannot understand father. I, too, plough, but my ploughing is different from theirs. I sow the seeds of *Hari Nam*; my heart is my fields and my mind is my plough, and God waters my fields. I plough both day and night, and I sow my songs.

Father : Why not have a village-shop and sit there and rest and sell merchandise ?

Nanak : Time and space are my shop, and I sit and deal in song. I praise Him who has made all this.

Father : None can understand what you say, your speech is so difficult. Why not enter again into the Government service, which is fairly easy ?

Nanak : I have already entered His service. I cannot serve another. I go whither He takes me and I do as He bids me.

At another time, when he met his mother after a long interval, the following conversation took place.

Mother : My son ! Do not go away now, but come and live in your house as of old.

Son : My house is His Temple, mother ! God is my home and His grace is my family. His pleasure is my utmost riches, mother ! He judges me not; He is kind and merciful as none else is. He blesses and blesses without end. He provides me with everything, and I am for ever happy in him.

Of what use is this life of houses, wherein a thousand desires consume the man; and there is no rest, neither in waking nor in dreams, mother ?

Mother : Wear clothes such as we wear; and be not so sad, so strange; go not away from us.

Son : My clothes are white and stainless, mother; for I live in love of Him who has given me so much love.

I am made to wear His Presence and His Beauty, mother !

He is my food and raiment.
The thought of Him, mother, is my covering of honou
His treasures contain everything.
My clothes are eternal youth,
I wear the perpetual Spring.
Of what use are these clothes, the wearing of whicl
    gives so much trouble ?
And then a thousand desires consume the man; and
    there is no rest, in waking or in dream.

Mother : Oh ! Why do you not live like us and eat what we
    eat ?

Son : I drink His very Presence, I eat of His precious
Substance, and partake of His Light.

In His glance is my heavenly sustenance. I have neither
hunger nor thirst. Of what use is this bread, mother, the
eating of which gives so much trouble ? And a thousand
desires consume the man ; and there is no rest, neither
in waking nor in dreams.

To the Hindus he said, "You are not Hindus"; to the
Mussalmans, "You are not Moslems"; to the Yogis, "You are
not Yogis"; and so was it wherever he went. He not only
withheld these names, but by his very presence changed
those that had borne them into men. When he left the place,
his eye seemed to be still upon them, keeping their minds
steadfast. A new life came to the people, in him they found
their God, their world, and their lost souls.

In him they began anew; and in him they ended.

NANAK AND HIS SISTER

When he prepared to go on his long journeys into the
trackless lands around, usually on foot, Nanaki (his elder
sister and his disciple) could not brook even the thought of
such a long separation from him.

She said, "O, divine one ! what will be our condition
then ? How shall thy lotuses live and breathe without thee !"

"Bibi," said the brother, "this is Heaven's call, I must go

whither it leads my feet. Many will attain the heavenly life
if you forego for a while your own yearnings. I would not
be gone from you. Whenever you will think of me, I will
be with you."

Guru Nanak did return to her frequently, interrupting
his travels.

Mardana, the rebec player, joined him; and Nanak took
up his royal residence under the stars.

He went to Sangaladeep and other isles in the south of
India, he visited the Nilgiri hills. He crossed the borders of
Assam in the east and the Trans-Himalayas in the north,
and went by Baghdad and Bokhara right up to the
Caucasian mountains. He visited Mecca, whither he came
by way of Baluchistan. He travelled throughout the north-
western frontier of India and the Kashmir. None ever
travelled so much with one single purpose; namely, to thrill
the earth from pole to pole with the working of his spirit.

NANAK AND DUNI CHAND

A banker named Duni Chand lived in Lahore in the
times of Nanak. He flew many flags over his house, each
flag representing ten millions. One day he came to see the
Master, and Nanak gave to him a needle, which he said he
would receive again from him in the world beyond this
after death. Duni Chand took the needle home, and told his
wife of the Master's strange speech, and still stranger
request to keep a needle for him in his books. Both went
to the Guru again, and said, "Sire, how can we carry a
needle with us beyond death, when all we have shall be left
behind ?" "Of what use is your all, then," said Nanak, "if it
will be of no use to you in regions beyond death where you
will have to pass long centuries ?" "Pray, then, tell us what
we can take with us," said they.

"The wealth of loving Him," said the Guru : "Hari Nam
will go with you."

"How can we have that wealth ?" said they.

"Just as you have this, if the Guru so pleaseth, if he giveth the gain of life, if he favoureth ye." said the Guru.

Both Duni Chand and his wife entered the path of discipleship.

NANAK AND A JEWELLER

The Master sat as usual under a tree, outside a city on the Gangetic plain in Eastern India. He gave Mardana a jewel, and asked him to go and get it valued in the city. None could value it truly; some offered gold for it, and some mere silver. Mardana at last met a jeweller, who, when he saw the Guru's jewel, brought all his jewels and offered them to Mardana, and said, "Who can pay the price of this priceless jewel? Who can buy Beauty? I offer my all for the joy of its auspicious sight. It is the beginning of my luck. It is the favour of God that I have seen it to-day." The jeweller Salis Rai and his wife followed Mardana and sought the refuge of the Guru. They were initiated into the path of discipleship.

NANAK AT EMINABAD

There at Eminabad in the Punjab, lived in those times, a carpenter who used to make pegs of wood and other implements for the village. He lived in "pure poverty," as the Japanese would say. His life was simple, his needs were few, and he was happy. He was a disciple of the Master, but full of natural simplicity. Nanak went straight to his house and lived with him for days. He neglected the table of the king and preferred plain bread and water at the house of this man of God. The king sent for Nanak and asked, "Why do you refuse my bread and eat at the house of a low-caste though they say you are a Saint?" "Your bread is blood and his bread is milk," replied Guru Nanak.

NANAK AND THE TANTRIK KODA

In a thick forest of India, Koda met Guru Nanak under

strange circumstances. Mardana had lost his way and fallen into the hands of Koda; Mardana was just what he wanted for his man-sacrifice. Koda bound him hand and foot, and began his preparations, lighting a fire under a huge cauldron of oil. The wind blew, the rain came, and the fire went out. He tried again with the same result; and he knew not why the elements went against him that day. He looked up and there stood Guru Nanak. His look disconcerted Koda, who went into his cave to consult his mirror. The mirror gave him the image of man, and he came out and asked for forgiveness.

Nanak said : "Koda ! Sing His great Name."
Koda entered the path of discipleship.

NANAK AND SAJJAN THUG

Sajjan kept a Moslem mosque and a Hindu shrine side by side for the weary travellers to rest in a lonely jungle pathway. There lay the bones of many a travellers that came hither to rest in the midst of the temple or the mosque. Once Nanak was the guest of Sajjan for a night. Sajjan served the Guru with the utmost devotion, for he took him to be a very rich man. He saw the sparkle of a million jewels on the Guru's forehead. Late at night, Sajjan, as usual, invited the Guru to retire to rest.

Such heavenly music was uttered by the Guru when Mardana began playing his rebec, that Sajjan was over-whelmed with remorse; he was washed with music. He cried, "Save me ! even me, O Divine One !" "Be pure," said the Guru, "and sing His Name !"

NANAK AND VALI QANDHARI

Once Nanak was near the ancient Buddhist city of Taxila. A bleak mountain now called Vali Qandhari (the prophet of Qandhar) stands with its bare peak at a little distance from Taxila, towards the Peshawar side on the

Grand Trunk Road by which came Alexander the Great
and other invaders to India. This mountain is so called
because in the times of Guru Nanak, there lived a Vali—a
prophet—a native of Qandhar, on its high summit. He had
built himself a house by the side of a little spring of crystal
fresh water on the top of the mountain. This was the only
spring of water near the place where once encamped Guru
Nanak and Bhai Mardana. Mardana was very thirsty. The
Guru asked him to go up and drink water from the fountain
of Vali Qandhari. Mardana went up, but the reception of
the Vali was very indifferent. "Who are you ?" said he. "My
name is Mardana, and I am a disciple of Nanak," replied
Bhai Mardana. "What brings you here ?" "I feel thirsty, and
wish to have some water from your spring." "There is no
water here for such as you; go back and ask your Master
for it." Nanak asked Mardana to go again, saying that they
were simple folk of God and wanted some water from his
spring. Mardana went three times as bidden by the Guru,
but to no purpose. The last time when he came back, Guru
Nanak said, "Never mind, Mardana ! Dig here. There is a
fountain of water flowing at your feet." The spring was
there, it came with its cool crystal waters kissing the feet of
the Master. Vali Qandhari, too, came down to see Guru
Nanak who so naturally attracted everyone. Guru Nanak
spoke to Vali Qandhari saying, "O friend, those who live so
high, should not be rock-like dry."

Vali Qandhari was enriched with the wisdom of the
Master, and blessed with poverty; he too, drank the waters
that flowed at the Master's feet.

KAMAL AND BRAHAMDAS ENTER DISCIPLESHIP

Nanak was in Kashmir, living in the forest near the
great lake. Kamal, a Mohammedan faqir, lived nearby on
milk that the wandering shepherds gave him; he was very
pious and sad, pining for the life of the Spirit. He pined for
that celestial goodness which comes to man only through
the grace of God. He was an old man now, and looked at

the setting sun and the rising moon with feelings as of a
beggar whom, when he came to them with his bowl, they
had turned out of doors. Brahamdas and Kamal were
friends; one an orthodox Brahman, and the other a Pathan
with glowing eyes. Pandit Brahamdas always had three
camels following him, loaded with volumes of ancient
wisdom. He always carried his stone-god hung by a thread
round his neck. Brahamdas informed Kamal of the strange
visitor to Kashmir who "wore leather and ate fish." He said,
"It is strange. Many a man who has gone and tasted the
nectar of his kindness is transfigured." Kamal, who had
been thirsty all his life, sought the presence of Nanak, fell
at his feet, and fainted with joy. As he rose, he found in his
own heart, the light which he had sought in vain in the
forests. Kamal followed the Master. Nanak asked him to
settle in the Kurram valley[1] (now the tribal frontier of
India), it was from here that the song of Nam spread
towards the West. Kamal was the servant of his Master, the
soldier of his King, a temple of holy song. Mardana entered
his final rest here; passing away in the great concourse of
the disciples of Kabul, Qandhar and Tirah, when Nanak
paid his second visit to Kamal.

Brahamdas wished at first to discuss his lore with the
Guru, and began thus :

Brahamdas : Where was God before Creation ? and how
    were things created ?

Nanak : He opens His eyes and He closes them, according
    to His pleasure. He knows.

Brahamdas : Who are you, who being a teacher of religion,
    wear leather ?

The discussion ended in a trance. Like dawn singing
through every leaf of the forests of Kashmir, came the
Guru's heavenly voice :

"Blessed is the disciple that hath met the Master !

He is gay as the face of earth adorned with flower and
    leaf,

---

1. Now in North West Pakistan.

He seeth this world, the garden of Beauty, in full bloom !
All lakes are brimful of nectar.
He is inly made divine and rich in colouring as a
    garment with madder dye;
The Mystic body of the Master has melted into his silver
    limbs.
And the lotus of life bursts in full blossom in the
    heartlake of the disciple.
The whole world cries as the antelope caught in a
    hunter's trap.
Fear and pain and thirst and hunger crowd from all
    sides;
But blessed is the disciple that hath met the Master !"

The Guru gave him the celestial vision. Brahamdas
entered the Path.

He was given the authority to distribute amongst the
folk of the Kashmir valley the Divine riches given him by
God.

NANAK AND A POOR MAN

(One of thousands of such who met Him)

Once Guru Nanak lived with a poor man. On leaving,
he burnt the poor man's hut, the walls and the thatching
of grass and all he had.

When the Guru came again, there was a palace for him
in place of the hut, and there was a bed of gold for him to rest
upon, when singing in ecstatic elation the Vision of God.

Whosoever met him, the Guru burnt his poverty and
his clinging thereto and made him rich.

NANAK AND THE LEPER

The leper was in his hut; and late at night the Guru
called him out; it was a moonlit night.

"Who is it ?" said the leper. The song flowed from the
Guru as soft loving light from the moon.

"It is but for a night, as the birds rest on the tree;
For at earliest dawn we go—no talk of me and thee !
A night on the roadside—a night and a day;
It is but as the meeting of travellers on their way !
Each noisy bird of passage from its branch its bearings
     takes;
Then every bough is silent ; we're flown as morning
     breaks !"

How could the leper believe that he could have a guest !
He came out and saw him. The song descended on the leper
as the moonlight clothed him with affection. Nanak said,
"When in the song of Nam we cry aloud, all our past
suffering is seen to come of our forgetfulness of the Beloved.
Suffering sets us on fire, makes us, as it were, red hot, and
cools us again, till we pass through a hundred fires !"

Nanak gave him the song and went away.

NANAK AND GOD'S HOUSE

Nanak the Master was at Mecca. The Master slept out
of doors with his feet turned inadvertently towards the
Qaaba, the House of God. The chief priest of the place came
and said, "O forgetful stranger ! awake and see your feet are
turned towards the House of God !"

The Guru replied, "Is it so ? Pray, turn my feet yourself
in the direction where the House of God is not."

It is here they asked the Guru, "Pray, tell us what does
your God eat and wear."

"Music is His food, and the colours of life are His
garment," replied the Guru.

NANAK AND TWO CITIES

Once Nanak was the guest of the City of Light, where
lived good people. At the time of departure thence, the
Guru cursed them, "Be ye scattered, and may there be no
city here." After a while the Guru was the guest of the City

of Darkness, where lived evil-minded persons. Nanak, on leaving the city, blessed them, "May this be your settlement for a long time to come !"

NANAK AND THE FOOLS

Once he was at Multan. Many false hermits lived there, and they were all afraid of some true one coming and disillusioning the crowds that assembled and worshipped them. They thought Nanak had come to deprive them of their living. It is said they sent Nanak a bowl of milk too full to have another drop, meaning thereby there was no room for him. Mardana wished the Guru to accept it, for he was thirsty and hungry after a long dusty tramp. He smiled, and returned the bowl, placing a little flower of jessamine on the surface of the milk. "There is room for me everywhere," said the jessamine flower.

NANAK AT HARDWAR

Some people were throwing water towards the Sun while they bathed in the Ganges. "O men ! what are you doing ?" said the Guru. "We are offering water to our dead ancestors living in the Sun," said they. At this, the Guru began throwing water in the opposite direction with both his hands. When they asked what strange thing he was doing, he replied, "I am watering my fields of wheat in the Punjab."

The priests of Hardwar collected round him and said, "Of what caste are you, and of what town ?" "My caste is the same as that of wind and fire, and I come from a town whence come both day and night."

NANAK AT KURUKSHETRA

During a great fair, the Guru was at Kurukshetra. He asked Mardana to go and get fire to cook his meals, and Mardana went and touched the fire of an "orthodox". The orthodox cried out in a rage, and fell upon Mardana;

whereupon the Guru said :

"The evil is still in his mind, hatred resides in his heart;
And yet his Cooking Square is pure !
Of what use are these lines of the Square when lowcaste
thoughts still sit with him in his mind ?"

NANAK AND EMPEROR SIKANDAR LODI

It was Sikandar Lodi, then Emperor of unfortunate India, who, along with others, put Guru Nanak in prison where he had to labour on the hand-mill. He did the labour; but the music flowed from him in the prison, and all came to listen, and all stood to listen in awe and wonder. Sikandar Lodi also came and stood listening, and asked forgiveness of the Master. The gates were opened, and for the sake of the Master everyone was set at liberty.

NANAK AT JAGANNATH

The priests of the temple began their hymn to their God. In a huge salver they put many little lamps of ghee, the pearls of the temple, and the offerings and incense; and all stood to offer it to God. There were priests that held each one a feathery *chowrie* (a ceremonial fan used for sacred rites, etc.) in his hand and stood at the back of the enshrined god to fan it. The priests began the ceremony, but the Guru paid no heed. After the ceremony, the priests were very angry with him. Then came Guru Nanak's voice like the voice of God, and all stood listening dumb as cattle.

Here Nanak sang his famous hymn, when the night was rich with her stars in full glow.

ARTI
(Hymn of Praise)

The whole Heaven with its myriad lights goes round
and round my Beloved !

The little stars are as pearls !
The winds fan him,
And there rises in His temple the incense from the
    hearts of a million flowers,
The endless music of creation resounds !
A million eyes hath my Beloved !
And yet no mortal eyes !
A million Lotus-feet are His,
And yet no mortal feet !
I die with joy of the perfume of His presence !
His Flesh emits a million perfumes !
And yet He hath no scent !
He is the Light of Life.
By the beams of His face the stars burn bright,
And He is the soul of everything,
My *Arti* is my waiting for things to be as He willeth.
When the master comes and stands by, the Divine Light
    is revealed !
The Moon of His lotus-feet draws me like a thirsty
    sarang whose thirst daily increases.
O God ! come and bend on me Thy saving glance,
And let me repose for ever in The Holy, Holy Naming
    Thee.

NANAK AND NUR SHAH OF ASSAM

Guru Nanak was in Assam in the city of Nur Shah, a
woman of black magic, who exercised strange powers over
all that locality. She fascinated and subordinated many by
her spells, compelling them to dance to her tunes. She
owned the whole country around, and many a mystic and
many a celibate and Yogi had fallen into her snare.

Mardana went into the city to get some bread for
himself, and he fell a victim to the machinations of the
slaves of Nur Shah. They fed him, worshipped him, but
"made him a lamb". They put him under their spell, and he
drank without water and he ate without bread. Mardana

was thus imprisoned in the spell of black magic of Nur
Shah, and could not return to the Guru. Guru Nanak went
to search for his Mardana, and found a lost disciple in Nur
Shah also. She came at last and renounced her magic at the
feet of the Guru. All her slaves were set free, and she
obtained her freedom in the song of *Nam*.

NANAK AND THE KING OF SANGLADIP

The Master went to the city of King Shivnabh. Shivnàbh
had been pining to see the Master. A disciple Mansukh had
already gone there from Guru Nanak's Punjab, and his
personality had stirred the surrounding country. The whole
royal family, after the King's years of sadness, entered the
path by the kindness of the Master. The mystic words once
uttered by the Master, here, are not fully understood as the
chronicles put them, but they are clear and most significant.
Shivnabh said, "Sir ! What do you eat ?" "I eat of men."
Shivnabh brought a man to him. "No, I eat of the son of the
king, not of a poor man." The king brought his own son.
The family collected together; the Master would verily eat
the prince—such was the wild thought they had of the
Master. The wife of the prince was addressed by the Master,
"He is yours, not of the king who gives him to me. Do you
agree to give him up ?" "Yes," said the princess; "with all my
heart if the Master wants him for his service." Nanak closed
his eyes, and all sat together in the sweetest rapture of *Nam*.
All were there and remained there, but when they opened
their eyes Nanak had gone ! He had "eaten" of the prince;
who was thenceforward a disciple, and not a king.

NANAK AND BABER'S INVASION OF INDIA

(Sung at Bhai Lallo's hut long before the invasion of Baber.)
    Listen, Bhai Lallo !
    Lallo ! I say, as He says to me,
    The darkness of Sin has spread around.

Both the Mohammedan and the Hindus are masks of
   Sin,
The Lie is sitting on the throne !
I see the Bridal Procession of Sin start from Kabul, and
   engulf the country in sorrow !
Lallo ! There will be sung a wedding song red with
   blood. And human blood will fall on the hands of
   new brides !
He alone knows how things come about;
But, Lallo ! a great calamity cometh !
The heaps of flesh-clothes will be torn into shreds !
They will come in Seventy-eight, and in Ninety-three
   they will go,
When He will rise—*the Mard Ka Chela*—the disciple of
   Man
And scatter the hosts of darkness,
And strike the False with Truth, and the Truth shall
   triumph at last !   *(Translated from Guru Granth Sahib)*

Nanak saw the massacre of Saidpur. Baber was march-
ing through the Punjab, and was ruthlessly destroying
everything before him. We have in *Guru Granth*, Nanak's
lament for his people and country, which he uttered on that
occasion :

I

"Save Thy people, my Lord !
Save them at any of Thy doors,
The soul of the people is on fire,
Send down Thy mercy, Lord !
Come out to them from any direction as it be Thy
   pleasure,
Save Thy people, my Lord,
At any of Thy numerous doors !"

II

"O, Master Divine ! To-day Khurasan is thine ! why not
   India ?
The Moghal, cometh as Yama towards India, and who
   can blame Thee ?

We only say it is the Moghal, the Yama, coming
   towards us !
O Beloved ! How many of Thy people have been
   brutally slain ?
Is it not all pain inflicted on Thy heart ?
Thou art the husband of all, Thou feelest for all !
If power strikes power, it must be witnessed in dumb
   helplessness;
But I do complain when the tigers and wolves are let
   loose as now, upon the herds of sheep,
O Beloved ! Thou canst not endure the tyrant of a
   conqueror that wasteth the jewels of life thus, and
   prideth himself on his power, seeing not his death
   nor what cometh after death.
O Master ! It is all Thy strange dispensation !
Thou bringest us together, and Thou severest us; in
   Thee we meet, and in Thee we separate from each
   other !
They call themselves kings, and they do as it pleaseth
   them;
But Thou seest, my Lord !
Thou seest even the little insect that crawleth, and Thou
   countest the corn he swalloweth with his little
   mouth !
A hundred blows of death come and strike, and yet the
   tyrant knoweth not Thy will !"

THE MASSACRE OF SAIDPUR

III

"There lie, rolling in dust, the honoured heads of the
   beautiful women of the palace; their hair-dressing
   still moist with perfumed wax, and the sacred
   vermilion-mark still wet on their foreheads !
The swords of Baber have clipped their heads without
   a thought, and their tresses lie scattered in dust, no
   one can say whose heads are these !

How strange is Thy dispensation, Lord ! How strange
  Thy visitation !

These women adorned the bright halls of pleasure once,
  and new brides sat with their bridegrooms.

And they were once swinging in swings of love, the
  lucky ivory bangles shook on their arms, and their
  feet made music as they walked.

There was a day when the old mothers of the families
  came and drank water after having touched the
  heads of the new brides with their golden vessels;
  drinking health and joy to their wedded life, and
  drinking all evil from off their heads—so great was
  the welcome given to them !

They ate dried grapes and nuts and dates, and their
  homes were resplendent with the leisure of passion
  and youth !

Today the same brides walk along the highways; their
  pearl necklaces broken, and halters round their
  necks; as poor mean captives led !

Youth and Beauty are deemed foes !

The mere slaves of Baber march them forth in utter
  disgrace and filth !

It is Thy will, Lord ! Thou givest and thou takest
  away

Thou rewardest and Thou chastisest as Thou willest.

O people ! If ye had not cheated yourselves in pleasure !

O people ! If ye had not turned your back on Truth !

The Baber's cohorts are rolling over the land now, and
  there is no escape !

The people cannot eat in peace, nor can they bathe nor
  offer food to their gods !

No women can sit and cook, nor anoint themselves with
  tilak on their foreheads !

There is no leisurely life now; it is all confusion and
  death !

They only see their ruined homes, their widowhood
  and orphaned life, they weep and cry and wail !

Ah ! what can the people do if such be His will ?
And who can be spared if it be not His will !

The Master and the Cohorts of Baber

The cohorts of Baber had razed Saidpur to the ground ;
and, as the Master says, there lay in the dust, the fairy heads
of the beautiful women, with their dressing of that morning
still moist with perfumed wax. He saw the sacred vermilion
parting on their foreheads—the auspicious sign of wedded
life—with feeling of a wounded father. He was unwilling
to leave the people that Baber's mad soldiery had taken
captive. He, too, was caught by them, and pressed into
service. They put a heavy load on his head, and his minstrel
was made a groom. The Guru called him and said, "Touch
the strings of your rebec, Mardana ! for the song comes
from Heaven. Let go the horse." The horse followed
Mardana, and Mardana followed the Guru, and the music
came as the shower of cooling rain to the thirsty people. The
miserable crowd heard the celestial hymns, and everyone
forgot his distress.

Baber came and listened and said, "I see God in the face
of this holy man !"

The would-be Emperor of India approached, and asked
if he could do anything for the Guru.

"I need nothing from you," said the Guru, "set at
liberty, if you please, these people, who have been
wantonly oppressed."

All were set at liberty forthwith.

Nanak and the Emperor Baber

Baber took Nanak to his tent and offered him a glass of
wine. "My cup is full," said Nanak, "I have drunk the wine
of His love !"

And these winged words of Nanak carried Baber away
to the celestial realms. The would-be Emperor of India saw

in His presence the true Empire of Pure Beauty. Never did a prince or a peasant meet Guru Nanak in vain !

NANAK AND MARDANA

Mardana was his Mohammedan minstrel. He first met Guru Nanak at the time of the latter's marriage. Mardana came and asked the bridegroom for a gift. The Master gave him the gift of Divine Song, and said, "Wait till I call you." Mardana was called, and he never left the presence of the "Bridegroom". When he died, his children took his place in the service of the Guru. To this day his offspring sing the Master's songs in the Sikh temples. But old love is passing; its place is not filled !

Mardana is the Master's rebec-player and companion, with all the wit and honour of the Punjabi Minstrel. Mardana is a blunt philosopher, "O Guru ! You live on Heaven's breath and whispers, but we men need food and raiment. Please leave these forests, and let us go to the haunts of men, where we may get something to cure hunger." The daily accounts of his hunger and thirst, related with all the confidence of his supreme love for the Guru, are genuine items of prayer which a child of man can utter to his God. After all we need no more than a loaf of bread now and then. The name Mardana was so much on the Master's lips that we cannot think of Guru Nanak apart from Mardana, playing by his side on his rebec. "Mardana, play the rebec, the music of Heaven cometh." This is the first line of almost every hymn of Guru Nanak.

Under the stars, under the trees, on the roadside, in forests, and on the eternal snows of the highest mountains in Central Asia, the Guru sang his hymns. In his discussions with the countless varieties of Indian and Eastern mystics and faqirs, the Hindu and the Moslem, the Yogi and the ascetic, the royal and the poor, in a thousand different studies of man and nature, in a deep association of silence with life and labour and love with death, the

Guru sang his soul out, as the rebec of Mardana played trembling beyond itself.

When Mardana is afraid, Nanak smiles and says, "Mardana ! have faith. Keep calm, see the works of the Beloved ! Wait and thou shalt see what God does."

NANAK AND HIS WHEAT FARMS AT KARTARPUR

Guru Nanak started wheat farms at Kartarpur, the town of Kartar (*Creator*) as he called it. His people came and worked with him in the fields. The Guru took keen delight in sowing wheat, and reaping the golden harvests : he was of the people. Once again his stores were open to them. The bread and water were ready for all at all hours of the day, and crowds came and freely partook of the Guru's gifts. All comers were filled from the Guru's treasury of thought and love and power; the diseased and distressed were healed by him.

He was an old man then; and he loved to see the crowds of God's disciples coming from the distant Kabul and Central Asia and Assam and Southern India—all the places where he had been in his younger days.

In the trackless world of that time, the old Father of his people travelled on foot, singing his Hymns of *Nam*, and gathering every trace of love. The Afghan and the Biloch, the Turk and the Tartar, the Sufi and the Brahman, the white and the dark races, mingled in his great heart. The disciples, both men and women came from all directions, and took part freely in the song of the Guru.

So great was the reverence of his own country for him, that Pir Bahauddin, the great Sufi teacher who counted his followers by thousands, one morning suddenly turned his back on *Qaaba* (which no Moslem would do), and began bowing in his *Namaz* in the direction of Kartarpur.

"Why so ?" cried his faithful followers, in alarm.

"This morning I see the light of God in this direction, my friends !" said he.

NANAK AND BROTHER LEHNA

(Lehna in our language means "the dues to be collected," and it also happened to be the name of a great man of the Punjab.)

Lehna was a flame-worshipper. There was a flame within his soul, so he loved nothing but flame. He would go up the Kangra hills to worship flame—the flame of the volcano : called, by the primitive villagers, the Goddess Durga, i.e., the lion-riding goddess of the great Hindu pantheon of gods and goddesses. The flame, as it came up from the volcano, seemed to leap into his soul, he burned more than ever with love of the Divine Flame. He was beautiful and godlike, a leader of the Durga-worshippers in those days. He would light for himself, while in the privacy of his sanctuary, a little lamp of ghee, and would watch the little flame for hours devotedly, and then, slowly rising, go round it in sacrifice, and suddenly begin to dance in rapture round the little flame. One day he heard of Guru Nanak, and the name fascinated him. He was on his way to Kangra, when he stopped to see the Master at the Town of God. Nanak asked him his name; and, when he replied that his name was Lehna, the Guru said : "Welcome, Lehna ! You come at last, I am to pay your *lehna*." After that Lehna never left Nanak. His companions, worshippers of goddess, went on their way, beating their cymbals and ringing their bells as usual. The flame of his little lamp in the silver plate waited for him at home, and departed with the night.

Beyond all expression was the love on each side between Lehna and Guru Nanak. The heights Buddha attained by his almighty struggle, Lehna attained through love. Lehna entered Nirvana in his love of the Master. Everything else that can be thought or seen, was very small for Lehna beside his love for the Guru. Nanak in this divine statue of love, chiselled his own image. He saw in it his eidolon, his transfigured self and bowed down to it.

THE SAFFRON-ANOINTINGS

Lehna was the son of a very rich man, and he used to dress in yellow silk of Bukhara. One day he came from his native place to see the Guru, and went to the field where the Guru was working. The Guru put a heavy load of wet grass on head of Lehna; who then followed the Guru home, the mud dripping from the wet grass and staining his silken clothes. As they entered the house, the Guru's wife said with great concern, "Sire ! see how his fine clothes are stained with mud !" Guru Nanak looked back and said, "Mud ! Seest thou not good lady ! He bears the burden of suffering humanity. They are not mud stains, they are the sacred saffron-anointings ! The Heaven anoints him, He is a Guru."

NANAK AND HIS DEPARTURE FROM THIS PLANET

The disciples and saints assembled. Bright was the day and beautiful the hour of his departure.

"Assemble, ye comrades,
And sing the Song of His praise !
Anoint the Bride,
And pour oil on her forehead,
And pray together.
The Bride may meet her Lord !
Guru Nanak left the earth amid a chorus of song :
"They search for the Master in vain
who search him on this earth,
The old father of his people is not to be found,
Neither in the grave nor in the cremation flame:
He is in the heart of Guru Angad."

Brother Gurdas, a disciple sang :

"Heaven heard at last the prayer of the people,
Guru Nanak descends on earth !
The disciples meet him and drink the nectar of his lotus
     feet !
In Kaliyuga (this dark age) we realize the Divine,

All the people are the people of God,
Guru Nanak makes all the castes one caste of man !
The rich and the poor combine in one brotherhood.
From this Founder of Humanity, a new race of love goes
    forth;
Nanak bows down to his disciple,
The Master and the disciple are one !
He is the Father of His people,
His song of *Nam* is our life for ages !
Nanak comes, the worlds are lighted.
Wherever the Guru goes, the golden temple of worship
    follows him !
Whatever mound or earth he puts his foot on is our
    Shrine.
The tree he sits under is our Temple.
The far-famed seats of Sidhas (*Yogis and adepts*) change
    their names, and the yoga-houses become the Guru-
    houses !
The temples of all the creeds seek refuge in him !
Humanity resounds with his hymns, and all is divine !
The Guru goes in all directions, seeking his own, all
    over the face of the earth;
He makes our hearts his gardens of love and peace,
And rivers flow in us singing his song !"

Another says :
"The dead rose out of their graves
As they heard the song of Guru Nanak.
He healed us all by showering on us the sparks of
    Divine Fire !
The veils were lifted up, and the disciples went freely ·
    in and out of the door of death, in concourse of song
    with the Immortals !"
Nanak the Master, sowed the seed of *Nam* in the hearts
    of men :
And the fields are ripe with the golden corn,
The harvests shall come, and the harvests shall pass,

But the seed is of God and is growing !
He gave him His own love, His own face and name and
  soul.
He gave him His own throne in the hearts of men,
Called him "Born of my loins," and made another
  Nanak on this earth !
This is Nanak the Master; the Spirit of God, that
  fashions Himself for ever in the image of man !
The harvests shall come, and the harvests shall pass,
But the seed is of God and is growing."

II

THE SECOND MASTER
ANGAD NANAK

Pilgrimage by the Old Nanak to the New

The last days of the Master, at Kartarpur were made bitter by the attitude of his sons towards bis beloved disciple, Angad. Nanak, as a spiritual teacher had given his love to his dearest disciple, and the jealousy of his family brought about a situation similar to that in the story of the awakening of Galatea. Nanak had therefore, already denied himself the pleasure of the presence at Kartarpur of his great disciple, on whom he loved to feast his mind, and had asked Angad to go and live at his own native place, Khadur. After this it was Nanak who would go occasionally to Khadur to see his Angad. A pilgrimage by the old Nanak to the new.

The Ecstasy of Love

One day, Angad, following Nanak, strayed too far out from Khadur towards Kartarpur; whereupon Nanak asked him to go no further, but to stay there and wait for his next visit. Angad stood looking at the back of the Master as he was slowly going towards Kartarpur, turning now and then to look back at Angad. When his luminous figure had disappeared, Angad saw it entering in his own soul. He felt bewildered with joy and wonder. There he sat on the roadside : lost in himself, his eyes fixed on the half-closed eyes of the mystical Nanak seated in his heart, his soul fast asleep in the Master's soul. Days passed in that ecstatic trance, the dust settled on his hair, and the tendrils of green grass caught his toes. So did Angad sit in a trance of Dhyanam, with nectar-tears flowing out of his closed eyes, till Nanak returned in haste from Kartarpur to see his mighty lover and his divine Beloved seated on the roadside. The Master strained him to his bosom; it was God embracing man. From such holy and secret confluence of the two Beloveds, the life of spirit flowed in a thousand shining rivers to the soul of the people.

ANGAD ON THE ROADSIDE

When Nanak left this earth for his original 'Kartarpur', Angad was left again on the roadside on this earth in the same state as when the Master had shown him how to bear physical separation in the union of Dhyanam. But Angad was deeply affected; he sought the lowly house of a humble disciple, and shut himself in a room, unwilling to open his eyes to look at anything else. His soul crane-like flew crying in the midair for his Beloved that had passed the limit of the sky. Months elapsed, and no one knew where was Guru Angad of the people. They hungered to see and to touch their Master, and thirsting crowds streamed hither and thither in the country searching for him. When Bhai Budha at last intruded on the love-Samadhi of Angad and persuaded him to come out to his people. Angad's first utterance was :

"What use is living on this earth
When the Beloved hath already journeyed on t ›
    Heaven ?"

And again he said :

"If a man melt not in submission to his Beloved, in vain
    doth he live, better his head were severed with a
    sword.
Of what use is life, if cherish not in me the pang of
    separation from the Beloved ?"

Angad, the second Nanak, has left us very few hymns of his own composition, but the few that have come from him are as brief and as intense as the two he first uttered on coming out of solitude.

I

Burnt be the fame, good name, wealth and rank, won
    at the hands of men of this earth !
Cast all such greatnesses into burning fire !
Of what use is all this if I have lost Him ?

II

My sisters ! it is the season of spring !
Such perpetual springs roll where the Beloved lives !
Praise Him, the beauty of Spring is His sign !

III

My sisters ! it is the Cloud-month,
And the clouds are gathering in the sky !
In this lover's month of joy, if I think of another, I die !
My sisters ! it is the *Sawan* month !
And it is raining love, it is raining joy;
To awake now is sin;
O let me lie in the embrace of my Beloved.
Wake me not, take me not from here, it is the sleep of
    peace !
O sisters ! it is the *Sawan* month !

IV

I was a locked temple;
The gems of God were stored in my heart,
And I knew not.
My Master opened the door of my heart for me;
My Master had the key, and I knew it not.
Now I see all.

V

Men with no eyes may or may not be blind,
But great is the blindness of him whose inner door is
    locked.

VI

The Nectar of which we hear is love of God.

Immortality for which we long is the song of *Nam*.
The secret of life is hidden in me,
But it opens in the kind Glance of my master.

VII

The way to the Beloved is unknown,
He finds whom He favours.

VIII

How can I tell you of Him Who knoweth and Whom
   none else can know,
Whose Will pervadeth everywhere and Whom the
   whole creation obeys ?
We come here sent by Him,
We go back called by Him;
His joy is goodness.

IX

The flag-bearers of *Nam* are great,
The singers of his *Nam* are rich
They have the key to the Door of Life
They are the chosen of God.

When Angad came out of his seclusion to the disciples,
(it is written) "The disciples saw in him the same aura, the
same face, and the same speech, as of his Master Nanak."
Born of His loins, there comes the Man complete !

From His eyes, a million more eyes take the flame of the
   Unseen,
Under his ribs throb a million hearts with faith and
   prayer,
His smile reveals the secrets of other worlds,
And the suns catch fire from the beams of His brow,
And the whole creation plays about Him in its original
   freedom, joy and peace !
Angad sings his Master's songs, which impart life to
   man, woman and child;
And he toils for his daily bread, making ropes out of the
   coarse fibres of the Punjab, sweating and singing.

The Playmates of Angad

Angad had little children for his playmates and companions. He always drew parables from the child mind to teach the great truths to his people.

He took interest in wrestling exercises, and was very fond of manly sports. Another delight was the education of young children. He formed a school round him for their instruction, and he simplified the old characters into a new alphabet, since called *Guru Mukhi*—"Learnt from the mouth of the Master."

Angad and the People

Angad had deep reverence for the people : the people were sacred. One day his minstrels refused to sing to his disciples, saying they were only for the service of the Master. Angad dismissed them, promptly ordering them never to come before him if they had grown so vain. When the minstrels obtained forgiveness of the people, it was only at the latter's intercession for them that Angad also forgave them.

Moths Round the Lamp

The Temple of Bread established by Guru Nanak was kept up by Angad. The whole people came to the new Master : some to be healed and blessed, others to be initiated as disciples. But, once they had come, they all continued, in one way or another, to hover round the magic personality of the Master, Angad, as moths hover round a lamp in the darkness.

Angad's Power

From Angad, the Master, spontaneously flew sparks of life, and the whole soul of a people caught fire from them. His creative power was shown in the raising of the dead by his presence. He worked in the Unseen, and lived more in the hearts of the people than in himself.

ANGAD AND EMPEROR HUMAYUN

Since the time of Baber, there was an attachment of the imperial dynasty to the throne of Nanak, the first Master, which continued more or less during the whole time of Baber's dynasty in India. This attachment was in the spirit of saint-worship that was so common in the Mussalman world, the belief being that the saints can avert many a calamity by their prayers.

Humayun was defeated by Sher Shah. He came to see Angad to obtain his blessing in regaining the throne, but Angad did not receive him. He was absorbed in play with children, and he heeded not Humayun who deeply offended at this "poor man's" reproof, put his hand on the hilt of his sword; but the sword refused to obey him, and his strength failed. At this Angad looked up smiling, and said, "Beaten by Sher Shah, you can do no better than strike a faqir with your sword. Better go back to your motherland before you seek to regain your throne."

THE THREE TEMPLES OF ANGAD

Angad reduced to writing the accounts of the travels and sayings of his Master, Nanak, as he could get them related by the disciples who had seen him and who came from far and near. He thus made a beginning of the gift of literature to the people, having at the same time given them an alphabet. In addition to the Temple of Bread and the Temple of Song, Angad the Master gave a third, the Temple of Teaching to his people.

ANGAD AND HIS DISCIPLE AMARDAS

Amardas was a spiritual genius of the times of Angad. He was a Vaishnava by faith, and a great pilgrim who had been forty times to the sacred Ganges at Hardwar—going there bare-footed, singing divine hymns all the way, and feeling charitable, good, pure and poor all the while. It was in the seventieth year of his life that a trifling event produced a revolution within him; merely the hearing of a song of Nanak sung by Angad's daughter, Bibi Amro, the wife of Amardas' brother's son. Once, early at dawn, she was reciting the song of Japji; uttering the Divine music as it is heard ringing through air from the throats of birds that are singing and soaring, while she churned butter for the family. The old uncle Amardas felt a solace in that angelic voice and a life in the song that he had never felt before, and he drew still nearer to listen to her. "Whose song is it ?" said he. "Our Father's," said she, "It is the Japji's song of Guru Nanak."

She took the old man to her father. Angad received him with the great respect that was due both to his age and to his position in society. Uncle Amardas, having seen Angad once, never while living, left his presence. Enraptured by it, Amardas would have died if it had been withdrawn. So deep and intense was his passion that he would find pleasure only in doing every service necessary to the Master; he would bring him a pitcher of fresh river water from the river Beas every morning for his bath, he would wash his clothes, he would serve him in the Temple of Bread—taking keen delight in self-effacement in his love. He extinguished his little self so thoroughly that he was considered mad; an old man who had no interest in life, he was dubbed Amru, and generally forsaken.

Even Angad, though sweet to everyone else, was not so gentle with him; for him there was all the rigour of discipline. The Master left the disciple alone to his ecstasies, to his labour of love, to his Samadhi; making response to him only in the Unseen, as the Master chose to cover his art-work under a thick veil from the vulgar gaze. Nevertheless, Uncle Amardas showed no annoyance at the treatment he received. Only once a year a yard of *Khaddar* (a coarse cloth) was given to him by Angad; and Amardas, not knowing where to keep the sacred gift, put it on his head and left it there. Where else could he keep it ? He found no place holy enough for it. Year after year he kept on winding over it the new cloth; and it so was for twelve years. Fond like a child of his Beloved, he would remain looking at him in a continual trance of wonder and joy and love. What else could he do ?

NEW CITIES SPRING

New cities began to spring round the name and person of the new Master. On the bank of Beas the disciples built a town called Goindwal, and they wished that the holy Angad should go and live there. As he could not go, Angad asked his beloved Amardas to go and make Goindwal his residence.

Amardas took up his residence at Goindwal; but he would come everyday, the old man, with a brass pitcher of the river-water on his head and the Ganges flowing from his eyes to bathe the Guru. He would come singing Japji all the way, and halt just for a moment's rest midway at the place where now stands our shrine : Damdama Sahib, to which pilgrims now resort, if only to look up to Heaven in hallowed memory of our great ancestors.

SAMADHI OF LOVE

While returning from Khadur to Goindwal alone late at night, Amardas never turned his back on Khadur. He would have died if he had turned his back on the Master even in that way. With his eyes looking still towards Master, he walked backward to Goindwal. Here, in this great old wayfarer who had travelled all his life with his face towards God, can be seen again in slightly altered form the Love Samadhi of Guru Angad sitting on the road to Kartarpur. Amardas had found his God; and, in deep spiritual contemplation, was unable to turn his back on the spot where He in His bright raiment shone.

The Disciple Crowned

One day, Amardas, while nearing Khadur with his brass pitcher of the Beas water, fell by the house of a weaver into his loom-pit, having tumbled against a wooden peg that the weaver had driven into the ground. It was a severe winter night, raining and pitch-dark. The weaver's wife disturbed in her comfortable bed by the noise of his fall, said to her husband, beside her, "Ah, who can have fallen at our door like that ?" The husband replied, "Who else could it be, but that homeless insane Amru; he, who never sleeps, never rests and never tires ?" This report reached Angad; the word "homeless" (Nithavan) used by the weaver, moved the Master deeply. He strained the old Amardas to his bosom; and from their meeting arose another sun in our sky, the new Amardas. "My Amardas ! my Amardas," said the Master, "is the home of the homeless, the refuge of the refugeless, the pride of the foregoers of their own strength. My Amardas ! my Amardas is the Master. Nanak himself !"

And he sent for five pice and a cocoanut in the fashion of Nanak, and worshipped Amardas, giving him thereby, a throne in the heart of the people.

III

THE THIRD MASTER
AMARDAS NANAK

THE POOR SERVANT

Datu, the son of Angad, was for a while, at enmity with Amardas. Once he proclaimed himself a Master at Khadur, but he was not accepted. At this, Datu, full of rage, went out to Goindwal, and kicked Amardas; having always regarded him as a poor servant of the family.

"What ! a servant of ours, made into a master ?" cried Datu. But Amardas only knelt down and began rubbing Datu's feet in deep reverence, "Sire," he said, my flesh is old and hard; it must have hurt your foot."

THE MASTER'S INJUNCTION AGAINST CASTE

No one could gain an audience of Amardas without first partaking of the Bread of Grace at the Temple of Bread. This Temple was now kept up by the Sikh Commonwealth; and everyday's collection of grain was milled and baked into bread and distributed free, reserving nothing for the morrow. If men were few and the bread more, the Guru was that day at home to the animals of the town : the cows, the horses, the bulls, and the buffaloes, were fed. If anything still remained, the good disciples took it to the river and feasted the fish with it.

THE HUMOUR OF AMARDAS

Amardas had a very happy way of receiving people for initiation. There is a beautiful life story of Bhai Menhga to be told. Menhga in vernacular means *precious*, and the Guru called Bhai Menhga meaning—one whom he had purchased at a very high price. One day, a disciple named Lal (meaning *ruby*) came for initiation. Amardas at once remarked : "O, you are a *Lal* of the Guru." Another day, a rich Mussalman horse-dealer named Allahyar came to the Guru merely to see him. But he became the Guru's slave when the shining glance fell on him and the Guru remarked, "Thou art Allah's *yar* !" (*the friend of Allah*). Ah ! it is difficult to be His friend. Come, I will make you the slave of God !" Allahyar entered discipleship. Later on this saint was known as Allah *Shah*......of God—the King.

BIBI BHANI

Guru Amardas had two daughters : Bibi Sulakhni, known as Dani; and Bibi Bhani who was the younger of the two. The latter, from her very girlhood, was fond of solitude and mystic thought. When playing with her girl companions, she used to recite the Guru's hymns and thus preserve her own spiritual atmosphere. She used to dress in a simple suit of coarse cloth (*khaddar*), as a poor girl, seeing which some of the Sikhs were displeased. One day one of them offered her jewels and silk dress to wear, and asked her to clothe herself as became her dignity. In reply to this she chanted a hymn of Nanak—"All this is illusion, and the wearer thereof too, illusion"; and she requested the Sikh to put all the proffered money into the sacred Temple of Bread for the service of the people. Bibi Bhani later on entered the path of discipleship; and she is one of the brightest among the heroic Sikh women who played their part in history.

THE CHOICE OF THE BRIDEGROOM

One day the mother conversed with the father about her daughter Bibi Bhani, "We must give away Bibi Bhani in marriage now," said the mother. "To whom shall we give her ?" said the father. "To a youngman like him," said she pointing at the same time to a youngman standing by. "Yes give her to him, then," said the father.

The youngman thus discovered was Jetha (*first born*). In this way the bridegroom was chosen; and, as he came to claim the bride, the Master said, "What gift do you choose, my son ? It is our custom to present a gift of your choice at this time : choose, therefore, my son; at my expense be your choice." "Sire, give me the jewel of *Nam*, give me the song of thy praise ." Here and thus did Jetha enter discipleship. He was married to Bibi Bhani; but, as poor as the bride and as spiritual as she, he began labouring, and thence forward continued as an humble disciple among a hundred thousand more who were digging the Guru Baoli (a well, with a staircase made of masonry leading down to the surface of the water). Jetha, like the others, carried baskets full of mud on his head, and surrendered himself wholly to the service of the Master in his love and Dhyanam, having renounced without repining all cares of the past and all anxiety for the future.

HOW THE FRAGRANCE SPREAD

A remarkable book, *Bhai Menhga* and *Mai Suhag Bai*, had recently been published (as tract No. 209) in the series of the Khalsa Tract Society, Amritsar. It is one of the truest pieces of Sikh history that has come to light—a history in a poem, as all true history should be. Bhai Menhga and his wife both yearn for the life of the Spirit, but are invariably defeated by ascetic ideas—"garbs of renunciation," till they despair of getting truth anywhere. And yet they cannot live without it. A stranger, a distant relative of theirs, comes on a visit to them. She makes herself perfectly at home with them, and looks after them as if she were the mother of the family. She cooks for them, serves them and lives as if she had thought : "Let me pour out floods of love, and efface myself." Since her arrival, that sense of acute despair which had come upon the household has been slowly vanishing. This kind woman has brought solace to them, but they do not know that it is coming from her. They notice that there is something in her life which she scrupulously hides from them. The more they think of her, the more imposing and mysterious in their eyes becomes this seeming-insignificant person. They find her acting as the mother of many orphans, and as the sustainer of many a poor girl deserted by a cruel husband—gambler, thief or drunkard. They find her sitting beside the wet and cold bed of a poor mother on whose starved bosom lies a new born babe, striving to suck. The wretched mother finds in her both a nurse and a benefactress, who washes her clothes, brings her new dress and food, looks after her children as long as she is confined to bed, and whom everyone in the house calls upon in need. They find in her a secret river flowing in a thousand channels, bringing water of life to the dead and the dying. They find her dumb about religion; she refuses to be defined, declines to be named—she desires only that some-one may catch the gleam of her soul and follow it.

She dawns as a gradual revelation on Bhai Menhga and his wife. Her every act is a prayer, her very step a song, and herself like the sky spread over the snow tops—as pure, as high. Things develop further and further. Once the couple fell dangerously ill. Twentyone days of a sort of typhoid fever and another fortnight of childlike physical weakness; but this untiring mother-servant of theirs is by their bedside, nourishing them with the milk of Love. Led by the grey lady, the couple go to Goindwal, where they join the holy army of the Guru.

Amardas had, out of the abundance of his generosity, given authority to 146 apostles of his to go and spread the fragrance in as many regions, and to preach the truth through the language of action in one uniform spirit of the Master; namely, in love and service of the people. Out of these 146 adepts, 94 were men and 52 women. Out of these 52 chosen women, one was Mai Suhag Bai, the Grey Lady, who had rescued the drowning couple.

JETHA

Ramdas or Jetha (as he was called), being the first-born of his parents, was from Lahore. Jetha's parents found him a moody boy, who would do nothing useful for any consideration. Driven by his people, Jetha was at last seen selling boiled pulse to the passers-by on a roadside near Lahore, where sometimes in his joy he would distribute the whole stock of pulse free to the hungry—an ideal pulse seller ! Finally, renouncing his native place, Jetha joined a party of Sikh pilgrims, and went with them to Goindwal. Soon afterwards he was discovered by the Guru's discerning eye; and thenceforth, Jetha never left the Guru's presence, whether the latter was making the rounds in his own country or on a journey to distant Hardwar. He was so selfless, meek, sweet and alluring, that the disciples began calling him by this original name Ramdas—which means Servant of God. After his marriage, he visited his parents with his noble bride; but he could not stay—he would die if separated from his Master. So he returned to Goindwal, and lived at his Master's feet.

THE JEALOUSY OF THE ARISTOCRATS

The prosperity of the disciples made the Moslem and Hindu priests and rich men very jealous of the growing fellowship surrounding the Master. A movement against him developed, and he was charged with wishing to make all castes one. By his teaching he had polluted, they said, the religion of his and their ancestors. Guru Amardas was accordingly summoned to the Imperial Court to meet the charges against him, but he sent as his representative Jetha, by whose frankness and persuasive advocacy, the storm-clouds were dispersed and the accusers abashed. All passed off well, but hatred rankled still in the hearts of the opponents.

THE MASTER AT THANESHWAR

The Guru went on the long journey to Hardwar to see his old friends and acquaintances; and, as he went, scattered the blessings of *Nam*. On his way he halted at Thaneshwar, where the people asked why he composed hymns in the unknown Punjabi dialect and why not in Sanskrit—the only language in which great truths can be expressed. The Guru said, "Sanskrit, now that is no longer the people's tongue, is like well water—sufficient for the irrigation of a small tract of land; whereas Punjabi, being the living language of the people, even if it be nothing but a dialect, is as the rain, which falls in showers all over the country."

AMARDAS AND HIS PEOPLE

Bhai Budha, seeing the coarse bread that the Master ate, while from his Temple of Bread his people were always feasting, said, "Why should we, your Sikhs, be so well fed, when you eat this coarse bread ?" The Master replied, "Bhai Budha, there is no difference between me and my people. I eat with their mouths, whatever you give them. That is my sustenance and not this coarse bread only." Jetha, standing by, was visibly moved, and burst forth in spite of himself into the song of praise :

"O Master ! Thou hast that abundance of Love for thy
    disciples which the mother has for the Child,
As waters are to the fish, we thy disciples are to thee !
Thou feelest the relish of the bread thy people eat and
    the taste of the water they drink !

As the cow finds her soul in the calf, as a bride finds it
in her bridegroom, so dost thou find thy joy in thy
disciple."

AMARDAS AND EMPEROR AKBAR

Emperor Akbar came to pay a visit to Amardas at
Goindwal. It is written, he got down from his horse and
walked a little distance bare-footed in his habitual reverence for all saints. The Emperor could not, however, be
shown into the presence of the Master before he had
partaken of the Bread of Grace.

The Emperor, having complied with this requirement,
obtained the audience he wished. It was on this occasion
that the Emperor offered to Amardas a large estate for the
Service of Bread. The Master declined his offer, and said,
"I have already obtained enough from my Creator. The
people are my lands and estates. Enough, that daily we get
our bread from God; we do not think of the morrow
Enough, that we are of the Poor, and think of the Beloved."
But as a token of his appreciation of the Guru's work, the
Emperor gave an estate of a few villages as a present to Bibi
Bhani; and this is the estate that later on was converted into
a flourishing colony of disciples, where today stands the
famous city of Amritsar.

AMARDAS AND JETHA

What Nanak saw in Angad, what Angad saw in
Amardas, Amardas saw in Jetha; who was the divine
Beloved of Amardas, and the story of whose discovery by
means of a happy chance (introducing him into the family
as a bridegroom) has been related. Bibi Bhani also had won
the heart of the Guru by her continued devotion; and she
prayed him that, to avoid all jealousy in the family, the
inheritance, as birth, of the Spirit of Nanak, should
henceforth, by his authority, be confined to her offspring.

The Guru conferred this favour on her; but the husband of the elder daughter was held in higher respect and the Guru felt that the people were opposed to his selection of Jetha. Accordingly, he sent for both sons-in-law, and required each of them to build him a platform for his morning and evening assemblages. Rama and Jetha set to their appointed work and finished it. The Master told Rama, the elder, that his platform was not well built and he must throw it down and build anew. Rama built it a second and a third time with no better result. The Guru continued to give the same orders to him till in disgust, he refused to rebuild it anymore. Jetha was treated by the Guru in exactly the same manner. He built and rebuilt the platform seven times, and each time with an increased joy and greater fervour; always falling at the Master's feet, imploring forgiveness, and pleading ignorance of the Master's exact requirements. When the platform was thus made ready for the seventh time, when the same joy was Jetha's and the same pleading, the Master strained him to his bosom, in an embrace as fervid and close as that in which Nanak held Angad. "Go, my son, as thou hast raised this platform seven times, so seven generations of thine shall receive in their soul, the spirit of Nanak and his high throne in Heaven," he said.

The Bridegroom Crowned

Amardas sent for his two sons Mohan and Mohri, and for Bhai Budha and other Sikhs. In this shining assembly of disciples, Amardas, having obtained five pice and a cocoanut, got down from his seat, placed Jetha thereon, and set the offerings before him, saying, "Thou art myself. The light of our Master Nanak is in thee." Jetha was acclaimed by the whole assembly as Ramdas, the Master.

Mohan resented this act of his father, retired in indignant silence to the solitude of his own room, and remained there confined all his life, voluntarily cut off from all society. Amardas then asked his younger son Mohri how he would look upon Ramdas?"Sire, to me, he is Nanak, Angad and thyself, in one !" said Mohri. Amardas, visibly moved by these innocent words, blessed the boy, and said, "Thou art my dutiful good son !" And Ramdas said, "O king of truth ! pray give the Master's honour to Mohri Ji, and grant me the honour of being thy devoted slave for ever and ever !" Amardas said, "I have given thee what was thine, and I have given him what was his. He is my poor good son, thou must take care of him."

IV

THE FOURTH MASTER
RAMDAS NANAK

RAMDAS AND BABA SRI CHAND

Baba Sri Chand, the eldest son of Nanak I, was the leader of a religious sect of his own. He roamed over the country as a mystic of great repute. During his travels Baba Sri Chand came to Amritsar to meet Ramdas. Seeing Ramdas's long flowing beard, Baba Sri Chand asked him jocularly why he grew it. "To wipe the dust from thy holy feet," replied Ramdas. "It is this magic that had made thee so great and me so small," said Baba Sri Chand.

RAMDAS AND AMRITSAR

Ramdas had selected a solitary place shaded by Acacia trees, part of the gift of land made by the Emperor Akbar, and at the bidding of Amardas, had laid there the foundation of a new colony of disciples. He left Goindwal for this place, and began digging a huge tank in which he proposed to erect a central temple for the Sikhs. It is the site where now stands the city of Amritsar. The work begun by him was completed by Guru Arjan Dev. It is written that here was discovered a water that healed many diseases. Following the Guru, many wandering Sikhs settled here. To this day, all the inhabitants of Amritsar approach Ramdas in prayer in all their difficulties and distress. So well chosen is the place and so greatly blessed by the residence of the Holy Ones, that Amritsar is not only the place of pilgrimage for the disciples, but an evergrowing centre for the trade and industry of the whole province. Its soil and climate are so different from the surrounding country that it can grow pears of Kashmir and peaches of Quetta along with the spices that grow in sub-montane regions. The whole city is surrounded by gardens of oranges and plantains, worked for profit; indeed today Amritsar is sending its fruits to distant marts like Calcutta.

A fruit-growing, a flower-breeding city of his Temple of Song : *Amrita Sar*, The Lake of Immortality !

RAMDAS AND ARJUN

Ramdas had felt his Beloved in his youngest son Arjun, and such was the prophecy of Amardas also. When Arjun as a baby, would crawl up to the plate from which Guru Amardas took his meals, the Guru would say, "Why so impatient, O little one ? Thou, too, shalt eat, from this plate."

Ramdas asked Arjun to go and live at Lahore till he should call him thence. This was a great spiritual pain for Arjun; but he was the soul of obedience, and prepared to go to Lahore. At his departure, his mother Bhani blessed the child; giving him her message of motherly love, which was put to music later, and which we Sikhs, treasure as the tenderest message ever delivered by a Sikh mother to her son :

"My son, let this be the blessing of thy mother; Forget not Him Whose Song renews our soul, and makes it clean of all dust; Whose love is our salvation.

Let this be the blessing of thy mother :

May the Master be merciful to thee, and, by His mercy, mayest thou always feel the Divine filling thy heart !

May His Grace be thy raiment and His Name thy food !

And honour come to thee direct from Him, and bliss without end flow from Him in thy soul;

Mayest thou drink nectar from the cup that is in His
   Hands, and may the cup be for ever thine.
Let this be the blessing of thy mother :
May no anxieties prey upon thy mind, and may His
   peace abide with thee !
And mayest thou like a bee abide in the flower of His
   feet !
My son, let this be the blessing of thy mother :
Mayest thou everyday be closer bound to thy Beloved !
May thy devotion prosper and thy soul shine in its own
   glory !"

THE DISCIPLE'S TIME OF EXILE

Arjun's exile was like to the exile of Angad from
Kartarpur, of Amardas from Khadur and of Ramdas from
Goindwal.

From Lahore he wrote his famous epistles to his Master,
which were intercepted by his elder brother and thus
withheld from the Guru. An epistle marked "3" reached the
Master safely, and Arjun was recalled from exile. On his
return, his father asked why he put the figure "3" on his
very first letter. The truth came to light; and Pirthi Chand,
his elder brother, was forced to produce the other letters,
which contained songs of supreme value. These were set to
music, and great was the rejoicing at Arjun's home-coming.

SONGS OF ARJUN

I

One moment, if I see Thee not, is like a dark age to me.
When shall I see Thee again, after so many days ?
Poignant is my sorrow as that of the *Chatrik* that cries
   for the rain-cloud ! -
Always thirsty and restless am I, O Beloved Saint, for
   the sight of Thee !

II

Fair God, how beautiful is Thy face, and how deep and
  sweet the melody of Thy voice !
Ages, not days, have gone by, and the *Chatrik* has had
  no drop of nectar.
Blessed is the land where Thou dwellest !

III

I pant for Thee, O divine Friend !
Passes not my night, my eyes know no sleep !
When shall I see Thee, O Lord ?

IV

(On meeting the Master)

Today breaks the morn of fortune for me;
I find today my Master, my Saint !
All-bliss is life; I have found my Beloved with myself !
No separation now, no pining, I am now for ever at His
  feet !
I am now for ever in His service !

THE SON CROWNED

It was on his home-coming from Lahore that Ramdas
embraced Arjun, and gave him the throne of Guru Nanak.
Ramdas placed the usual offerings before Arjun, and Bhai
Budha gave the Tilak of spiritual kingship. Ramdas said,
"Arjun has today become the Master of the whole earth; the
light proceeds from his throne and lights the worlds."

THE POETRY OF RAMDAS

The poetry of Ramdas flows like a stream of love whose
cooling melody yearns for the Beloved, and sings of the
magic spell of His glance. It is put in the mouth of the Bride
of God, who pines in her longing for one more glimpse of
Him, and still one more ! The Master's divine music thrills
the soul of a whole people, and his song makes everyone
pure.

V

THE FIFTH MASTER
ARJUN DEV NANAK

THE BOOK OF THE DISCIPLES

Arjun Dev conceived the idea of enshrining song as the Deity of the new Sikh temple commenced by Guru Ramdas and completed by Arjun Dev. Accordingly, the Guru collected the hymns composed by his four inspired fore-runners, and composed many more of his own. He called the collection, "Word of the Master"—later *Guru Granth*—and placed it in the Hari Mandir as the book of the people. He used to chant the life Mantrams everyday, morn and eve, with the tambura accompanying under the touch of his fingers with his heavenly voice, and the disciples gathering and listening to his divine songs, in wonder and enchantment. Lovely music flowed from under the dome of Hari Mandir and was absorbed by its walls and the waters of the surrounding lake. To our own time, it echoes and re-echoes in that sacred place.

THE TARN TARAN

Arjun Dev built another great temple some twelve miles away from Amritsar, and called it Tarn Taran. The soil and climate of this place also are so blessed that it has a healing effect on bodily sufferers. Tarn Taran is a name which means the temple "whence people swim across the Sea of Ignorance to save many a drowning soul."

Hari Mandir

The colony at Amritsar grew everyday, and became the Sikh centre of spiritual humanity. Akbar had already ordered a large plot of land round the colony to be made revenue-free. The Temple attracted the thinkers of that day; there, mystics like Mian Mir, the unknown spiritual ancestors of Inayat Shah and many others met with the greatest of all, Guru Arjun Dev. A close study of the literature created by Moslem saints like Bulleh Shah (the disciple of Inayat Shah), Shah Hussain, and others, reveals the spiritual influence of that age. The first significant departure made by the Moslem saints was that they began to sing in Punjabi, a practice due to the Guru's influence alone. With him began a general renascence, in which the greatest share was taken by Moslem thinkers—so much so that we find Shah Hussain singing his own version of *Guru Granth*, and the tempestuous song of Bulleh Shah ringing with the music of joy of Hari Mandir. But, behind this literary awakening there was a still deeper aw   ; of the divine idea in the life of the Punjab, as disti   ied from the mere academic intellectual assent to Tru

As of old, the Hari Mandir (the Golden Temple)   till held in reverence by the seers and mystics of the Punjab, who alone can appreciate fully the effect of this place and its associations. Only the "living ones" know this secret influence of the Temple. A great Vaishnava Faqir came from Bindraban, and was so impressed by the clear spiritual aura of the Golden Temple that his Dhyanam passed from Krishna to the Master of this temple, and he never left it. A Mohammedan adept residing in the Western Punjab can never pass Amritsar in a railway train without alighting and paying his homage to the Hari Mandir. He says, so wonderful is the link between earth and Heaven here, that even now, after the Guru has been personally absent for hundreds of years from his temple, the place still possesses that old enchantment. The "extinguished ones" are rekindled, the broken made whole, so mighty is the remaining effect.

Isolated by a sheet of blue water, with heavenly song resounding day and night, the Temple seems immune from worldly trouble, whose dust and smoke can never touch its pearly surface. All initiates and disciples here feel a solace unknown elsewhere. The other day the French artist M. Jarl spoke to us of the effect of the Golden Temple on him. He said the light seems to come from within the golden dome of the Temple, and it is this inner light that kindles the whole prospect around it. The sky is its roof and the four cardinal points its doors. The sacred waters wash its walls, which stand so firm on the sea of Maya.

There is no doubt that in the days of Arjun Dev, this Temple was the favourite resort of the aspirants to the spiritual life; thither they came to dip their torches in its light, that they might fill the land and its heart with the gleam that M. Jarl saw. The fresh vigour and inspiration that flooded the land, can only be traced to the heart of the Guru. If history has not shown it yet, it is because it is not old enough. Only when the dry details are forgotten does history begin to find the invisible evidence of the work of its real makers in the songs and sayings of the people.

THE SIKH EPOCH

The Sikh was the creation of the mind of the Sacred Masters; he was wholly new Consequently he was bound to leaven the Hindu and Moslem civilization that lay in ruins before him. He stamped the mind of the age with his image.

THE COMPOSITION OF GURU GRANTH

Arjun Dev saw that interested people were passing compositions of their own as those of the Masters. He had already decided to give an authentic history of the mind of the Master in his song. But the manuscripts of the first three

Gurus were in the possession of Mohanji, the son of Guru Amardas, who had cut himself off from all society and would see nobody. Bhai Gur Das tried to get the manuscripts from him but without success; Bhai Budha also was unable to get access to him. As without these manuscripts the task was hopeless, Guru Arjun Dev himself travelled to Goindwal, to endeavour to persuade the recluse. On arriving, he dipped himself in the sacred waters of the river where the great Masters, Amardas and Ramdas, had bathed many times before him and fell into a trance of love as he sat again on the spot where his elders used to sit. In this trance Guru Amardas appeared to him and said, "Blessed is thy purpose of composing *Guru Granth*. Thy song is powerful to melt the very stones into waters." Arjun Dev, feeling blessed by the Darshanam of the great teacher, proceeded barefoot, 'tambura' in hand, to where Mohan dwelt in self-absorption ("Mohan" means "the inspiring God"). The true king of the people sat in the dust of the street in front of Mohan's dwelling, and sang these hymns to the accompaniment of the 'tambura' :

I

O Holy One ! Thou hast charmed my soul,
Thy palaces rise aloft the shining cities of Celestials before my eyes !
And at the Palace door stands a whole universe to adore thee.
O Love ! Thou dwellest beyond thought,
The silence of wonder steals on me, as I see thee appearing suddenly in the assembly of saints singing at thy door !

(This song roused Mohan from his sleep; he opened his window, looked down, said a few bitter words and disappeared again. The Guru sang another hymn.)

O Merciful One ! bestow on Thy humble creatures Thy mercy, and bliss them by rolling down floods of Glory on Thy servants !

O Formless Beloved ! pray, appear before me, and by
the beauty of thy countenance fill this moment with
Eternity !

Come from everywhere, O Fascinating One ! and satiate
me with love !

II

Eternal One, beyond all price are Thy words of passion !

Blessed, blessed, are the ears that have heard Thy
melody !

Honey-sweet, honey-sweet is Thy speech !

O Great Mohan ! Thou art renunciation, Thou art
samadhi, Thou art bliss.

Thou hast heard God's word from His lips, thou art the
blessed perfection.

The secret of love hides in thy bosom.

I, too, take refuge in His palace at the door whereof all
creation awaits His mercy.

O Holy One ! Thou hast made the starry heaven and
Thou wrappest Thyself in it.

(Mohan was appeased, and came down to receive the
Guru. The Guru again touched his 'tambura , and sang.)

O Beloved ! which is the way to Thy presence ?

All see Thee, but few find the way of thy adoration.

They are made immortal whom Thou inspirest with
knowlegde of Thyself.

There is Immortality in a single glance of Thine.

In Thee is the life everlasting, in Thee is all refuge !

When I see Thee, O Love ! I am all pure.

There is all wisdom for me in Thy fragrance.

O Sovereign mine ! reign for ever on the throne of my
heart; on me for ever bestow Thy commandment and
from me for ever accept service !

(Mohanji delivered the manuscripts to the Guru. The
Guru raised the manuscripts to his forehead in deep
reverence; then, feeling happy with them in his lap, he
again lifted up his voice in song.)

God bless Thee, Mohina ! Mohina ! Mohina !
The race of man is saved !
God's Word goes to the people, blessing them and
    bestowing immortality on them.
This is the staff on which the old and the miserable, the
    starved and sick, shall lean in their distress, and
    obtain solace.
My house is full of the light of the song of life today !
People of God ! come, assemble, live in this light;
    dissolve this song in your soul !
Rejoice and partake to this immortal feast !
O Beloved ! the dead shall rise with life, if Thou castest
    Thy glance of pleasure on them !
The disciples wonder at the miracle of Thy handicraft
As Thou revealest Thyself to them !
Thus both day and night did Arjun Dev give forth
    celestial muŝic, and thus did he pour his soul on the
    joy-astonished land of the Punjab.
The Hari Mandir at Amritsar is his holy shadow.

ARJUN DEV AND HIS PEOPLE

News would come that pilgrims to Hari Mandir were
on their way from Kabul or Qandhar or other distant places.
The Master would ask his noble consort to prepare a simple
repast for Guru Nanak's children that were coming.
Dressed like a peasant in a black woollen blanket, the
Master would go out of Amritsar barefooted, his wife
accompanying him with a basket containing bread and
vegetables; and both would wait on the roadside for the
disciples who came along singing the hymns of the Guru,
and growing in number as they approached Amritsar.
Arjun Dev would welcome them, as the mother distributed
bread and water Thus served, the disciples would say,
"Great is Guru Nanak; great is Guru Arjun whose disciples
have so much faith in their hearts, and so much service in
their hands."

Akbar came to see the Golden Temple, its architect, and its deity, more than once. It is stated that when Akbar asked the Master, as was his wont, the way to acceptance by God, Arjun said, "The way to Him is through His favour and inspiration. It does not need to pass through the mosque of the Moslem or the shrine of the Hindu. They reach the goal who love." Akbar wished to make a contribution towards the upkeep of the Golden Temple but the Guru declined the offer, on the ground that the temple must be supported by the people. As the Emperor insisted on doing something for the Guru before he left the Golden Temple, Arjun said, "There is a severe famine in the country, and it would be best if thy imperial visit were to be marked by the remission of this year's land revenue to the poor farmers." Akbar gave orders accordingly.

Arjun Dev as Husband and Father

Arjun Dev, prophet, poet, composer of music, passionate lover of the people, architect, saviour, was intensely human. He was a loving husband and an affectionate father. Mata Ganga once in his presence expressed a wish that her son should hasten to her from Heaven, he having already been so long a time upon the way. Arjun Dev said to her, "O dear one ! your son would come, but he is waiting for the call to go forth from Bhai Budha. It is he who will call your child from Heaven to you, at some auspicious moment when he is in a happy mood." She was to go and ask Bhai Budha to pray for the birth of a son to her. Accordingly, she took offerings and went, attended by a number of female disciples, seated in a bullock cart. As the party approached the abode of Bhai Budha, the ringing of bells, the creaking of cart wheels, and the unusual bustle,. caused a flutter in Bhai Budha's cloister. His cows took flight, breaking their ropes. Bhai Budha inquired somewhat angrily, who was flying in such haste thither ? The old seer was still ruffled when the aspirant to motherhood placed her offerings before him. He said, "O mother ! I am only a grasscutter of the Master's house. I am a slave of his slaves. How can there be anything so compelling in my word ?" She returned home and related to Arjun Dev what had happened. "It *must* be so, O good lady ! one day," said Arjun Dev, "The saint has foreseen our flight from Amritsar, and it must come to pass. O Good lady ! you ought not to have gone to see God's holy man in that way. Do as I tell you. Prepare a simple meal with your own hands, singing the song of Nanak. First mill the flour in your hand-mill, knead it with honeyed milk of Nam, and then take this sacred song-bread to the disciple. Take no dainty dishes with this bread; just a little salt and a few onions in the fashion of the Punjab farmers—this will be the homely meal he loves."

She did so. Bhai Budha, who had received the Divine Gift of Nam from Nanak, was now an old man, with a silver-white flowing beard and all-white locks; but under these snows, his face was still aglow with the Divine, and his deep transparent eyes were brilliant with the fire of Heaven. When the woman appeared with that simple repast for him, the old man began lisping like a child whose feelings are fresh from Heaven, as he began to eat. "O Mother ! he said, "thy son will be the Master of Masters. He will be the king of his people. He will break the power of the Moghals as I break these onions under my fist. He will be the temporal king of his people. The people will gather round his throne. He will wear two swords, the sword of Heaven to save his disciples from the arms of death, and the sword of Earth to save his people from the Moghal oppression. Mother ! thy son will appear as the sun comes on the dark worlds."

Arjun Dev was very fond of the child that came thus from Heaven at the blessing of Bhai Budha. The baby was named Har Gobind. The baby came by a prayer, and Arjun prayed when he was born.

Har Gobind fell ill. The Guru had an anxious time; and,

as the child recovered, he melted in a song of thankfulness. We read this song in *Guru Granth* : "Thank God, Har Gobind is well again !" The enemies of the Guru's house tried to poison the child; but their plan was frustrated, and the child was saved by a fortunate incident. On this occasion again, a hymn was sung by Guru Arjun Dev, as we read in *Guru Granth*, expressing his joy at the miracle which saved the child.

The Guru was all prayer. Every little event of his private personal life was the act of Heaven for him. His whole body and soul trembled in his Master's hands as the *Sitar* strings trembled with music in his own. He uttered only living music, whether private or public in life. He poured forth his songs and vitalised all those who came in touch with him by his lyrical power. His inclusion of private hymns, embodying his feelings as a father and a husband, shows how greatly he valued these emotions, esteeming them as divine as any. Nothing in the whole range of the religious literature of India surpasses these simple hymns in their deep sincerity and intense human interest. For the first time a Teacher of *Brahma Vidya* harmonises the personal and the impersonal in his self-expression.

ARJUN DEV AND HIS BROTHER PIRTHI CHAND

There is a story of the strange reply Ramdas made to a disciple's question as to the nomination of his successor. "He who can, by his presence, melt even wooden hearts shall be my successor," said the Guru. The disciple went and sat near Pirthi Chand and heard him chant Japji, and he went and sat near Arjun Dev and heard him sing Japji. He returned and said, "O Master ! I pricked the wooden legs of the bedstead on which Pirthi Chand sat reciting Japji with a needle, but the needle broke. Again I pierced with a needle, the wooden legs of the bedstead on which Arjun Dev set reading Japji and this time my needle pierced the wood as if it were wax."

Pirthi Chand never could forget what he regarded as the injury inflicted on him by his father's withholding from him the throne of Nanak. He was always on the look out to injure Arjun Dev; and he often succeeded in inflaming the Moslem priests of the neighbourhood to raise a clamour against the composition of *Guru Granth*. He organized a deputation of the Maulvis to represent to the Emperor Akbar that the book was full of blasphemies against both the Hindu religion and the Mohammedan. Of course, the Emperor, who knew Guru Arjun Dev very well, dismissed the suit of the Moslem priests. But this family-jealousy continued smouldering in the breast of Pirthi Chand and his family.

ARJUN DEV AND THE PRINCE KHUSRO

The Emperor Akbar died a few months after his last visit to the Guru, and Jehangir became Emperor of India. This was a period of political tumult. Prince Khusro, who had been many times to see the Guru with his father, came flying for his life from Jehangir and his ministers, to ask the Guru for pecuniary help which might enable him to return to Kabul. Guru Arjun Dev received the prince very kindly, and, moved by his pitiable condition, gave him five thousand rupees, which would take him safely to Kabul. This private act of kindness was interpreted by the Guru's enemies, headed by Pirthi Chand, as a serious political crime against the then Emperor of India. They informed Chandu, the Hindu Minister of Jehangir, an old enemy of Arjun Dev, who had obeyed the mandate of the people in preference to complying with a request from Chandu that his daughter be accepted as the bride of Har Gobind. It happened thus : Chandu, as it was customary, employed his Brahman priest to find a suitable match for his daughter. The priest came, and offered to betroth her to Har Gobind; but the disciples gathered, and said that the Guru must not consent to this alliance, as Chandu was a traitor.

The Guru saw that his refusal would increase the fire of
racial jealousy against his person; but he firmly obeyed the
voice of the people, and declined the offer. Chandu, though
deeply offended, tried in various ways to make up the
difference; but the Guru would not be moved out of his
resolve.

Chandu, therefore, stirred up the jealousy of the Court
against the Guru. The latest weapon to his hand was
supplied by Pirthi Chand and his associates. A friend's act
in helping another friend was exaggerated into serious
sedition and rebellion against Jehangir; as if the Guru, with
the help of Khusro, intended to overthrow Jehangir. At last
the machinations of Chandu succeeded in inflaming the
Emperor; Guru Arjun Dev was summoned, and appeared
before Jehangir at Lahore. Before leaving Amritsar, he had
installed his son Har Gobind as his successor, and he took
leave of his devoted wife, as if for ever. When the Guru
came into the presence of Jehangir, it was evident from his
mere appearance that he was no sedition-monger and
contemplated no harm. Jehangir, therefore, received him
with great consideration. The interviews continued for
some days; and Chandu was ceaselessly active, so that at
last the Emperor was forced to ask the Master why he
helped Khusro against him ? He replied, "Khusro was in
distress; he appealed for help and the Guru helped him.
It was a man helping a brother-man in trouble, and not
an aid to rebellion against you, the king. Khusro was flying
to Kabul and he has gone there." The Emperor ordered a
fine of two lacs to be paid by Arjun, but the Guru firmly
said, "The money I have is not mine. It is collected by the
people, for the service of the people, and I have no private
money out of which to pay you this fine. But even I had,
I would not pay any fine, seeing I have done no wrong."
It is stated that the composition of *Guru Granth* formed the
subject of a second charge framed against him, on the
grounds already mentioned. Jehangir, therefore, asked the
Guru to alter the hymns so as to bring them into line with

orthodox opinion. The Master replied, "I acknowlegde no earthly king in this matter. The true King has inspired these hymns, and they are informed with the Spirit of God. I cannot alter the sacred word. It is destined to stand by itself, and needs no support of any other scriptures. The sacred book contains nothing but the song-chants of the Glory of the Highest; at Whose high door wait a million prophets, from Whom all cometh out, and to Whom all return." Jehangir, it seems, handed over the person of the Guru to Chandu, on the latter's promise to recover the fine without unnecessary molestation. But this promise Chandu never meant to keep.

ARJUN DEV THE POET PROPHET AND PEOPLE'S KING

The last days of Arjun Dev can be imagined, now that the character of his captor has been made clear. He was kept prisoner in Chandu's own house; where, in strictest secrecy, he was made to suffer unthinkable tortures from day to day. Burning sands were poured on his bare body, he was compelled to sit on hot iron sheets. And, as he would take nothing from Chandu's house and his Sikhs were never allowed to come near him, the Master was starved. In the daily routine of torture, Chandu allowed short intervals when he went and asked the Guru to accept the alliance with his family that had been proposed, and thus to release himself from prison. He made no reply. The Sikhs were eager to pay the ransom and to rescue him, but he had forbidden payment of unjust fines. Mian Mir heard the tale of sorrow, and came to see him when it was late. Mian was indignant on seeing the condition of the Master, and wished to move the Emperor for his release. But the Master calmed his mind and asked him to look up. As Mian Mir looked up, he saw the whole Heaven gathered around his head and the Angels forming a canopy over him with their wings. In strong contrast with his anxious disciples, the Guru was calm, undisturbed, full of ineffable peace. Mian

Mir bowed down, and left in silence. Arjun had accepted tortures for his people, who must be made strong to stand for justice, to suffer and to die for truth they love. Mian Mir saw the great idea and kept quiet. At last Chandu made up his mind to kill Arjun Guru by suffocating him in a fresh cow-hide, in which he was to be sewn up, when he asked to have his bath in the river Ravi. He was led out in prisoner's clothes to the river, whose waters in those days washed the walls of the Lahore fort. The Sikhs saw the Master; who looked at them, still forbidding all action. "Such is the will of my God; accept it," said he; "Move not; stand calm in your injury." The Master never returned to the prison, the body was given to the river Ravi. He left the earth, singing Japji, as crowds of his disciples stood calm but deeply afflicted, looking on.

VI
THE SIXTH MASTER
HAR GOBIND NANAK

THE AFFLICTION OF THE SOUL OF THE PEOPLE

Arjun Dev was cruelly tortured to death, to the sore affliction of the soul of the whole people. The devotion they bore to their Master was deep and selfless. While they helplessly witnessed his cruel death, a curse arose from among them, both against the Moghal Empire and against themselves. Now that He had been tortured, of what use was life ? Their prospect was annihilation : acceptance of which meant the eventual disappearance from this earth of the type of spiritual humanity created by the Master; resistance to which meant sorrow, suffering, hunger, and death for themselves and their children—but, so great was the love of the people for their true king, that all these ills must be endured. So great was now their indignation, that they felt everything they held dear—religion, song, home, love of child and wife—must be sacrificed, and their love for the Guru redeemed. For the first time in the centuries' long enslavement of the Indians by the hordes of barbarous invaders from the near West, there was resistance. Guru Har Gobind, driven by the curse and prayer of the people, unsheathed his shining sword, and declared a holy war against the unrighteous Empire of India. The fire that had come leaping from outside into the camp of peace, must be quenched.

Ignorance of the preceding events had led many to

believe that Guru Har Gobind waged a war of hatred
against the Empire, thus compromising his ideals of
spiritual Humanity, which were of a life at peace with all
creation. It is commonly forgotten that the Guru's heroism
that appeared in his character, at this juncture, was not a
herosim that kills and murders, but the heroism that dies
with a glad heart. It is akin to the heroism of the Sati-
woman who dresses herself in the most passionate colours
when her husband and lover is dead. It certainly seems
incongruous that her self-adornment at that moment
should be one of joy and not of mourning; yet those
beautiful colours are nothing but the symbol of that flame
of devotion which will lead her presently to leap into fire
that consumes the body. A similar pure resolution came to
the whole Sikh people and to their leader, after the cruel
death of Guru Arjun Dev. There was the distinction of
military uniform, the wearing of two swords, the riding on
a charger, the defiance of mighty powers; but how few they
were, and was it not all the pathetic preparation of a Sati ?
This is the spirit of the Guru's declaration of war; the rest
is mere dusty detail. Here out of the roots of life rises a new
Bushido, a pure passion for death in love.

As of old, Bhai Budha, the hoary-headed saint, placed
before Har Gobind the *Saili* or Ribbon of Renunciation that
Nanak wore and gave it to Angad, who gave it to Amardas,
who gave it to Ramdas, who gave it to Arjun Dev. Har
Gobind said to Bhai Budha, "No, give me two swords to
wear instead." He saluted the Saili and put it by. The Master
ordered all his men to wear swords, to keep horses, and to
make arms : determinig to take his disciples through blood
and fire, since they wished it. When the command went
forth, the disciples were already prepared; and they began
bringing offerings of arms—arrows and swords and shields
and bows to the Guru. The Sikh people was thenceforward
dyed in passionate colours like the Sati-woman, and the
whole Sikh world courted death in a spirit similar to the
spirit of Yamato of Japan; that is, not proposing to

themselves any clear purpose, sacred or otherwise; but merely for the love that would not suffer them to live in inactivity and submission.

Alarmed by the new pomp of Har Gobind's court a few of the worldly-wise proffered counsel both to Mother Ganga and to old Sikhs like Bhai Budha, that the Master should be persuaded not to adopt a dangerous militancy. Mother Ganga replied, "He is on the throne of Guru Nanak. His ancestors are with him. My son and his Master can do no wrong. All this is as Heaven ordaineth." Bhai Budha, moved by the same counsellors of peace, again sought the presence of the Guru, to tell him that these warlike preparations would draw the wrath of the whole empire on their heads, and thus annihilate the Sikh nation. In reply, Guru Har Gobind merely looked at Bhai Budha, who bowed down, saying, "Thou canst never err. All is right that thou doest." The Guru's mere glance intensified Bhai Budha's reverence, rejuvenated his faith, and rekindled the passion of his youth. Bhai Budha, left behind when Guru Har Gobind went from Amritsar, knew no rest; he breathed prayers to the empty air, conjured up the form of the Guru in imagination, and in Hari Mandir at his feet, singing love songs.

News of those doings soon reached the Emperor Jehangir. Chandu, the arch-enemy of the Sacred House, was still busy. There was now a good deal of evidence for a charge against Har Gobind, of rebellion. The refusal by Arjun Dev to pay the fine imposed on him, was remembered. Guru Har Gobind was at last summoned by the Emperor to Delhi. He came, and saw, and conquered Delhi by dint of his natural majesty. He began living in Delhi as the Emperor's guest. Whenever Jehangir went out into camp, there was a separate tent and camping ground for the Guru.

The False King and The True King

We treasure a beautiful story of a Sikh of Agra who was a humble grass-cutter. The tents of the two kings being

pitched side by side in the fields, the poor Sikh approached
Jehangir's tent with an offering of two copper pice out of
his wages, and desired to know where was "the True King"
"Whom do you wish to see ?" said Jehangir. "I want to see
the True King," said the grass-cutter. "I am the king," said
Jehangir. The grass-cutter placed his offerings before him,
bowed down to him, and rose and said, "O True King ! save
me, thy slave, from this sea of darkness, and take me into
thy refuge of light that is All Knowledge." On this the
Emperor told him that he was not the king sought, and that
the saviour's tent was pitched yonder. The grass-cutter
hastily took back his offerings, and went running to the
Guru.

The queen, Nur Jehan, took a deep interest in the Guru,
and had many interviews with him. Also, with the poor
frequenting the place, he was in much repute as a comforter.
During these days, Jehangir fell ill; and, following the
barbarous advice of his Hindu ministers, he invited his
astrologers to tell him of his evil stars that brought illness
on him. These astrologers were heavily bribed by Chandu,
who was always seeking to detach the Emperor from Har
Gobind. The astrologers accordingly, prophesied that a
holy man of God should go to the Fort of Gwalior and pray
for his recovery from there. Chandu then advised the
Emperor that Har Gobind was the holiest of men and
should be sent to Gwalior. Jehangir requested Har Gobind
to go; and though he saw through the plot of his enemies,
he left for Gwalior immediately. While Har Gobind was at
Gwalior, great was the distress of his Sikhs in Delhi and at
Amritsar, who suspected foul play at the part of Chandu.
In fact, Chandu did write to Hari Das, the Commander of
Gwalior fort, urging him to poison the Guru or kill him in
any way—and promising a large reward. Hari Das was by
that time devoted to the Master; so he laid all these letters
before him, who smiled and said nothing. The Guru met
many other Rajahs who were prisoners in this fort, and
made them happy.

When Jehangir at length recovered, he thought of Har Gobind again. Undoubtedly, Nur Jehan, who evinced a disciple-like devotion to the Master, had something to do with his recall from Gwalior. However, the Guru would not go unless the Emperor agreed to set all the prisoners in the fort at liberty. The Emperor at last gave way; and, on the personal security of the Guru, all the prisoners were released. The Guru was hailed at Gwalior as *Bandi Chhor*— the great deliverer who cuts fetters off the prisoners' feet and sets them free. There remains, in the historic fort at Gwalior, a shrine of the *Bandi Chhor Pir*, worshipped by Hindus and Mussalmans alike, where they have lit a lamp in memory of the event, and where a Mohammedan Faqir sits in hallowed memory of some great one of whom he knows only the name—*Bandi Chhor*. In the Punjab, in the daily prayers of the Sikhs, Har Gobind is saluted as *Bandi Chhor*. Surely he carried this name from Gwalior to Amritsar !

HAR GOBIND'S RESPONSE TO THE DHYANAM OF HIS DISCIPLES

In Kashmir, there lived a poor old Sikh woman named Bhag Bhari. She was a great saint, and lived in complete dedication to the Guru. In the year when Har Gobind was busy fighting near Amritsar with the forces of Shah Jehan, in a small skirmish, when Shah Jehan was only an heir apparent, this old woman, in her perfect Dhyanam, made a shirt of coarse cloth with yarn spun by her own hands. She stitched it herself; singing all the while, the songs of the Beloved, and deluging the cloth with Dhyanam of love, as it trickled from her eyes in tears of ecstasy. "O God ! Will my Beloved come and wear it ! Will he honour his slave ? O, how can he come this way ? My Beloved, come to me now ! These eyes are now to close for ever. May they once more behold Thy face !" Nameless feelings of love rose and sank in her veins. The garment was ready for the Master.

He left the fight, and rode his charger with haste to Kashmir, knocked at her door, and said, "Give me my shirt; good lady !" With tears in his eyes, he donned the shirt of coarse cloth, as she had wept all those days for a glimpse of him.

This response of Har Gobind to his disciples' inmost prayers and Dhyanam was continuous and unfailing. We read of his answer to the Dhyanam of a Mussalman lady, the daughter of a Qazi of Muzang—a suburb of Lahore, which was at that time provincial capital of the Punjab. A woman of great spiritual power, while a girl, she had become versed in mystic lore as it was preached in that neighbourhood by a leader of the Sikh-Moslem school, Mian Mir. Through Mian Mir, many followers of Har Gobind had already paid their homage to them. Wazir Khan, the influential Minister at the court of Emperor Jehangir, was one of the devotees of the Guru. The case of this great Mussalman lady was beset with exceptional difficulties. Her devotion for the Guru knew no bounds; even Mian Mir could not suppress her divine flame, but was forced to help her to find the Guru. By temperament she was the heroic soul, absolutely sincere and unworldly. No amount of prudential advice to conceal her spark of life by burying it deep in her bosom could prevail with her; she would live at his feet or die. She would express her Sikh opinions with the utmost frankness; openly she condemned the hypocrisy of the Mussalman; she praised the Master, and sang of his beauty and his saving love. Finally, she was condemned to death. But her inner gaze was fixed on her Master, and she knew he would come. Har Gobind made a daring response to seek her at night, took her from a window of the Qazi's house, with his own hands, and (like an intrepid lover) carried her off to Amritsar.

Come what may, let the kings be against him, and let the worldly-wise renounce the Master. Let it be ridicule, public shame or even death—the Master must rescue his disciple. Kaulan is her holy Sikh name. The Guru provided her with a separate house; and, while she lived, he extended to her his hospitality and kept her secure, under circumstances of great peril and difficulty, from the injury that comes to such as her from religious fanatics. Every morning the Master would go from the Golden Temple to Kaulan to nourish her soul with the Darshanam for which she pined day and night. The Master was a pilgrim every morning to the temple of her love.

Sain Das, a devout Sikh, built a new house in his village near Ferozepur, and would not occupy it unless the Master came and graced the room prepared for him. "Why not write to the Guru to come to us ?" said his wife, who was sister to the holy consort of the Guru. "Oh, he knows all, what is the use of writing to him, when he hears the prayers of our hearts ?" said Sain Das. Thereupon, Har Gobind at Amritsar felt the divine pulling of the love and Dhyanam of his disciple, and went to him.

On this very journey, the Master went right up to Pili Bhit on the borders of Nepal in response to the love of a Sikh saint, *Almast*—the "God-intoxicated" man.

The Sikhs left behind at Amritsar felt very keenly the pang of separation from the Master. Headed by Bhai Budha they commenced a divine service of Dhyanam. Every evening they would light torches and go in procession round the shrine, feeling the Master to be with them. On his return, he told Bhai Budha how this devotion had attracted the Guru to the Golden Temple every evening. He blessed them, saying that the night choir organized by Bhai Budha would abide for ever at Hari Mandir, and that he should always be with it. The Sikhs still lead this choir round the Temple in his hallowed memory.

Har Gobind and Shah Jehan

Through the kind offices of Nur Jehan, Mian Mir, Wazir Khan, and others, Jehangir was induced to cause no injury to Guru Har Gobind or his Sikhs, in spite of the efforts of

Chandu's party. But these had begun to inflame the mind of the heir-apparent Shah Jehan against the Guru, especially after that open skirmish with the hunt party of Shah Jehan near Amritsar. Jehangir died suddenly in Kashmir, and Shah Jehan became Emperor of India. Shah Jehan must fight with the Guru, as the Guru had already openly challenged him. The various engagements between the Imperial forces and the disciples of the Guru, cover the whole life-time of Har Gobind. The Sikhs always fought with a superhuman courage, and the Emperor's armies were worsted in all these affrays. The Guru finally left Amritsar and went to Kartarpur, and, after giving battle there, retired to the submontane parts of the north-eastern Punjab, where his son had already founded a town called Kiratpur. It is near this Kiratpur that Guru Tegh Bahadur later on purchased a site for his residence which he called Anandpur; it provided a solitary retreat free from all outside disturbances.

Engaged in warfare with the Emperor of India, and liable always to be attacked unawares, Guru Har Gobind was never at a loss, never in haste, never afraid of results. The date of the wedding of his daughter, Bibi Viro, coincided with the first battle of Amritsar between the Guru and the Emperor. While the rest of the Guru's family escaped in time, his daughter Viro inadvertently remained on the upper floor of the house, which by nightfall was besieged by the Emperor's troops. Bibi Viro stayed alone undaunted in the house, and kept silent. When she saw a rescue party of the Sikhs coming, she refused to accompany them till they showed her father's rosary. She was then safely conveyed to the place where the rest of the family had taken refuge. While this turmoil was on, the Guru ordered that the wedding of his daughter should be duly celebrated that very night in a village at a distance of about seven miles from Amritsar, which was accordingly done, amid great rejoicings. Only at the bride's departure was the customary pathetic note struck, in the father's farewell message to his daughter. A daughter's marriage, with us in the Punjab, is full of rare pathos—surrounded as we have always been by danger and political turmoil. And the Guru's message to his daughter is full of the tenderest feelings of a father towards his daughter.

THE MASTER AND HIS DISCIPLES

Thus he was, almost simultaneously, celebrating his daughter's marriage and busied with the grim business of fighting a hard battle and running to the rescue of his wounded disciples. Of this very time, it is related that two of his disciples were lying in blood, and that he went to them, wiped their faces, gave them water to drink, and caressed them, crying like a father, "O My Mohan ! O My Gopal ! Tell me what can I do for you ?" They replied, "O Master ! the proof that God is, is that you are here. It was our prayer to see you with our eyes now closing for ever." "God bless you my friends," said he, "You have crossed the Ocean of Illusion."

Still yonder at Kartarpur, on the river Beas, where she had been removed for safety, Kaulan lay ill. Her burning soul of love could not stay on earth in separation from her Master. Separated from him, she fell dangerously ill. Har Gobind found time to pay her a visit and, as he sat by the bedside of his heroic disciple, she passed away. Singing in the soft music of her closing eyes, the prayer of thankfulness, she fell asleep in the very arms of God.

There was yet another great soul waiting for him at his village, *Ramdas*, near Amritsar : Bhai Budha who was preparing to leave this earth. Har Gobind hastened to his side. Bhai Budha's whole soul leapt with joy on beholding the Master before beginning his last journey. The Guru said, "Bhai Budha, thou hast seen the last five Masters and lived with them, and thy realization is great. Please give me some instruction." The Bhai replied, "Thou art the sun and I am only a fire-fly. Thou hast, out of thy infinite mercy, come to see me and to help me swim across the Sea of Illusion. Touch me, touch me with thy hands, and bless me, O Master mine ! Thou knowest all. Thou art the spiritual and temporal Protector of the holy. Thou art God, we all know; but how thou playest the part of a holy man in these days, only God knows. Sustain me, and let me pass Death's door without suffering. Sustain my son Bhana, too, when I am gone and keep him at thy feet. Help me, O Lord ! O Saviour of thy disciples."

"Thou hast already entered the Realms of Immortals, brother !" said the Master, as he placed his hand on the forehead of his old disciple; and Bhai Budha passed on.

Where Har Gobind could not go, he made response in Dhyanam; and, in fact, this response was continuous and unbroken amid all struggles of the outer life. Manohardas, a great saint, the great-grand-son of Amardas, died at Goindwal. The Master plunged into deep prayer for him. As he came out of his samadhi he said, "Mano-Har—stealer of the heart ! Triumph ! triumph for him ! Great saint of God !"

Har Gobind sent an invitation to Anand Rai (King of Joy), the son of Mano-Har of Goindwal. Anand Rai came; and Har Gobind put his shoulder under the palanquin on which Anand Rai was riding, and bore him a little distance. Anand Rai alighted, and bowed down saying, "Why dost thou treat me with so great a kindness ? I am naught but the dust of thy holy feet. What if the bamboo grass grow very high ? It can never equal the fragrance of the sandal-tree."

"Without service of his saints, man is a barren rock," said the Master, "In the service of his saints, he is God."

Har Gobind, though hunted by the imperial hordes and continually liable to sudden dangers from them, was always calm and collected. When Painde Khan, once the trusted general of Har Gobind, whom the latter had brought up from boyhood as his pet cavalier, turned against him, went over to the side of Shah Jehan, and reappeared as leader of a hostile army, the Guru rose early as usual, and sang Japji and Anand songs. As he was chanting hymns and praying, his Sikh generals came in hot haste to inform him of the approach of the Moghal forces. The Guru said, "Be calm. There is nothing to be afraid of. All comes as our Creator wills." Once Painde Khan engaged in a pitched duel with Har Gobind. The ungrateful Painda uttered profane words to the Master, who replied, "Painde Khan, why use such words when the sword is in thy hand, and I give thee full leave to strike first ?" Painde Khan, bending low, aimed a sword-blow at the Master, who avoided it. Again Painde Khan struck with similar result. Gobind was trying to play with his old and beloved servant, and, if possible, to awaken in him his original sense of fealty. But Painde Khan grew more and more angry and desperate; his attack became deadly and Gobind dealt a blow under which he fell. From this blow he regained his old sense of discipleship; and, as he lay dying, the Master took him in his arms, thereby readmitting him to grace. The death of Painde Khan is one of the most pathetic scenes in the life of Har Gobind. As he sat shading Painde Khan's face from the sun with his shield, he addressed him lovingly, "—O Painde Khan, thou art a Mussalman, repeat thy Kalma now, for thou art dying." The fully-awakened Painde Khan replied, "O Master ! from thy sword has already flowed into my mouth the Elixir of Immortality. Master, thy sword-cut is my Kalma now !"

Har Rai, his grandson, always wore a heavy gown and once as he was passing through Har Gobind's garden, the folds of his flowing gown struck a flower, which fell down, torn from its branch. The Master saw this, and said to Har Rai, "My son ! always go about with due care, lest you disturb the slumber of union of some blessed ones, and tear them away from God as thou hast torn this flower from its branch." Har Rai thenceforward, all his life, gathered the folds of his gown in his hand wherever he went.

Har Gobind found in Har Rai the spirit of Nanak; this

time in a more subtle and mystic form, and it was at Kiratpur that the Master gave his throne to him and left for his heavenly abode.

It is written by the Dhyani disciples who were present at the time of the departure of Har Gobind Sahib from the earth, that the face of Heaven flushed rose-red and that they heard the soft singing of a million angels in the inner firmament in one spiritual concourse of joy.

The Master, before giving up his body, said, "Mourn not; rejoice in that I am returning to my Home. He who obeys my word is ever dear to me and in the Guru's word is his beatitude. Fill yourselves, O disciples ! with the song of His Name, and live immersed in its ever-increasing inebriation divine."

VII

THE SEVENTH MASTER
HAR RAI NANAK

After the passing of Har Gobind a calm ensued, for the Sikhs were, by nature, peace-loving and fond of celestial contemplation, and the Guru's residence was now permanently shifted from Amritsar to Kiratpur—an out of the way, inaccessible place. Besides, Emperor Shah Jehan had seen, during the lifetime of Har Gobind, that it served no good purpose to make the Sikhs his enemies. On the illness of Dara Shikoh, his youngest and most beloved son, the Emperor sent a conciliatory letter to Har Rai, and asked for his blessings. But not many years had passed, when Shah Jehan fell a prisoner into the hands of his son, Aurangzeb, who also killed his brothers and usurped the throne of Delhi. Dara Shikoh fled in fear of him, and sought refuge with the Master, being already imbued with the mystic lore of saints like Sarmad. The Guru received him kindly, and filled him with that solace which no fear of death can disturb. Dara Shikoh was eventually caught and beheaded at Delhi, and Sarmad shared his fate.

Aurangzeb then turned his attention to Har Rai; but instead of adopting violent measures for his capture, the Emperor sent him a polite invitation to visit Delhi. Har Rai refused to go to Delhi, but sent his eldest son Ram Rai to represent him there. Ram Rai effected a compromise with the Emperor, and yielded on many points to the advice of Aurangzeb; with the result that the latter tendered his political patronage, which was accepted by Ram Rai. This news of the moral weakness of Ram Rai reached the Guru, who ordered that his son should never come back to see him. "Let him go whither he pleases", said the Master, "he is not my son, when he has compromised the gospel of Guru Nanak."

Har Rai had an exceptional seclusive mind; he loved quiet and did not mix very freely with people other than his disciples. He had military discipline for himself in everything that affected his conscience. As said elsewhere, he never plucked a flower or a leaf in his life; his room was the temple of peace.

One day during a ride, he halted at the door of the cottage of a poor farmer. It was not the hour of the morning at which he usually break-fasted; yet he called out at that door, "Good woman, bring me the bread you have prepared for me." The woman, half wild with joy, brought out some coarse bread, which he ate while still in his saddle. The disciples were astonished at this departure from his iron discipline in such matters, and next day as they rode they brought the meal at the same hour. He laughed, and said, "My friends, it was no hunger that caused me to beg the bread, but the song of love and Dhyanam of which it was made, and which obliged me to go there to accept it. It is seldom I get such bread. I pine for my disciple more than they pine for me. I am pulled by the strings of love that my disciples sometimes snatch from the Hand of God. God is Love."

Har Rai sat love-fettered in one posture from evening till almost daybreak, breaking the usual engagements of the evening. When he found his attendant Sikhs eager to know the cause of this having sat in one posture as if there were fetters on his feet, he said to them, "Brother Sikhs ! Brother Gonda of Kabul in a trance fell at the feet of the Master, and love fettered them by his child-like clasp. How could the Guru rise till the disciple rose out of his trance of Dhyanee love ?"

VIII

THE EIGHTH MASTER
HAR KRISHAN NANAK

The child Har Krishan, the younger son of Har Rai had developed those mystic signs by which the Master was always recognized. The very Darshanam of Har Krishan healed the sick and comforted the miserable. Har Rai bowed down to this child as to Guru Nanak, and left the earth.

Ram Rai began conspiring against the child Guru at the Imperial Court at Delhi, and finally succeeded in getting him summoned there. Like his father, Har Krishan was averse to seeing Aurangzeb. At Delhi, though he was ordered many times to see the Emperor, he persistently refused to do so. Finally he fell ill in Delhi. This illness of Har Krishan is to us, his disciples, in the nature of a protest.

Har Krishan was a mere boy, they say, when he came to Nanak's throne. But is not genius independent of age ? A little later in our history, did not Gobind Singh a boy of nine, occupy this very throne at the time of a miraculous re-creation of a whole people ?

When Har Krishan lay ill at Delhi, his august mother, at his bedside, saw that he was thinking of his coming death. "O son, why art thou turning thy thoughts away from this earth so soon ?" she asked. "Be not anxious, mother, for me," said the Guru, "my safety is in His will. I am safe wherever He may take me. Mother, be not anxious; youth or age matters not. Does not Arjun Dev say,

'The Master is the Reaper of His crop; it is His pleasure, and sometimes He reaps it while green and sometimes when golden ripe ?' Know, mother; what our God does is best. Has not the Master, Nanak said, 'What pleaseth Him is good ?' "

The family-jealousy was blazing then at its full, and many blood-relations of the Guru were setting themselves up as "Masters". Guru Har Krishan, though very ill, sent for five pice and a cocoanut, and bowed down saying, "Baba Bakale" (*Baba Nanak is at Bakala*). The Boy-master felt his spiritual responsibility for the people, and named the place whence Guru Nanak would come to his disciples once again. None else had the celestial vision that could see as Har Krishan saw. Naming Guru Har Krishan is the cure of all diseases.

IX

THE NINTH MASTER
TEGH BAHADUR NANAK

"Baba Bakale"—He is at the village Bakala ! Many impostors, distant blood-relations of the Master, proclaimed themselves the new Nanak. But the trained disciples well knew the fragrance of the soul that comes from the true Beloved. They soon found their Master. So great was the joy, that a disciple, Makhan Shah got on top of a house and cried in ecstasy to the heavens and the earth, "Guru *Ladho* ! Guru *Ladho* !" *The Master is found ! The Master is found !*

Tegh Bahadur had lived till now in extreme abstraction and in awful solitude. None could go near him, such was his reserve, inaccessible as the high peak of a mountain. His Dhyanam-abstracted look disconcerted people; and they passed him by, called him "Mad Tegha."

Till now, we have seen that every reincarnation of Nanak that has shown before us was different and yet alike. Tegh Bahadur could not bear the sight of creation without a deep agitation of soul. He could not but suffer from a profound sadness on seeing the helpless destiny of man's life imprisoned under the "Inverted Bowl" of this blue sky. He could live in the Dhyanam of the Beloved, and nowhere else. So sympathetic, so saddened by the world's distress was he, that he would have died of sympathy, had he not been put in the centre where shines the light of the Beloved. If God had not caught his mind in the magic net of His own

Effulgence, if Tegh Bahadur had not found peace in the spirit of Nanak, his temperament would have led him to be one of those who sacrifice themselves. He would lay down his life to save a poor cow from being led to the slaughterhouse, in order to escape the pain of the great illusion.

Tegh Bahadur always sings the sorrows of created life, and converts them into a vision of Heaven—a joy of self-realization. He finds joy nowhere but in His Nam and praise, and he exhorts everyone to be of that spirit. "Do they not make ropes of wet sand on the river bank, who rely on the riches of this earth ? Like a picture painted on waters, like a bubble on the wave is not all this magic of evanescene unsatisfying ? O Man ! thy supreme vocation is to live in the Beloved !" Tegh Bahadur's note is Renunciation : he dwells only upon the nearness of his Beloved, and the enlargement of the divine Idea in human life. The pleasures of life are so many pains; but, as Tegh Bahadur says, all realization of truth and its joy springs from these hard pains. Shed your tears for the sorrows of the world, but make them into a rosary for telling the beads of Hari Nam.

Sorrow is your wealth, suffering your gladness of soul, if you are really great as he himself.

Your optimism is austere and ascetic, and never can be reconciled to life but in Him.

Tegh Bahadur's mind is ever awake. It alone is made for ever free of the drowsiness that the Maya of life induces in everyone. "To forget One and to feel enamoured of another reality, is Maya," says the Master. "You shall sleep not, O Bride ! if you have chosen to wait for the king tonight." Tegh Bahadur's emphasis on this aspect of the Dhyanam of the disciple is as great as that of the older Nanak, judging by their songs. "O Brother ! Nothing in this world can be thine for ever; therefore think of Him alone, and live retired from the sorrows of life. Plunge yourself again and again into thought, and see what the world contains that can promise aught but the illusions of magic colours, snaring you again and again without purpose. Therefore, turn within and see the truth within yourself."

Guru Tegh Bahadur was so tender in his being, that he ought not to have been allowed to come in contact with the suffering of the people. His poems are tears shed for them in the silence of his heart. Soft as a raincloud, his songs awakened the dry hearts of men.

"Forget yourselves, O people, but forget not the Beloved. Forget not, in your gifts, the great Giver." Such is the message for Tegh Bahadur; which, sinking deep in the heart, makes life painful, but delicious. It makes men sleepless, but full of the peace of the infinite. Tegh Bahadur's word bestows on us a repose which no death can shake. It is the greatest solace ever uttered of the Sikh martyrs ! What reck we of this earthly life ? We lay it down for a higher life that put forth its signblossom in the Window of the Soul ! Nothing matters. What are fetters to our feet, when we see wings already spread for our soul to fly to the Beloved ? What is torture, or death, or wrath of kings, when to our inner ear the angels are already singing victory ? What injury can fire do us, or waters, or swords, when we see beings made of light take us in their embrace and support us in a faith that we are His and He is ours and all is made of light and song and joy ?"

TEGH BAHADUR AND AMRITSAR

The seat of the Master and the disciples, as we said, had shifted to Kiratpur; and Amritsar was already in the hands of impostors, priests who saw the money to be got by priest-craft at Hari Mandir. When the Guru had gone towards the hills, the disciples also departed thither and only priests remained behind. Since the time of Arjun Dev, there had sprung up a kind of civic administration, which collected the offerings of people at large for the up-keep of the Sikh cities, temples and tanks. Often the administration got into the hands of people other than the disciples, though everyone was eager to call himself a Sikh in those halcyon days. For some time the civic administration worked well; but later the surrounding enemies of the House of the Master came in and enlisted as Masands or collectors of offerings, and made the whole administration inimical to the disciples. They afflicted the true disciples in many ways, and the disciples endured without a sign of murmur all that came from Masands in the name of their Beloved. A full revelation of their ill-doing was made to Gobind Singh in a drama played before him at Anandpur, and it was he who abolished the Masand administration and destroyed the tyrants.

The signs of this tyranny were visible when Tegh Bahadur paid a visit to Hari Mandir. The priests shut the doors of the temple against the Master, and he said, "The priests of Amritsar are men of blind heart that burn in their own lust of greed." But, as the news spread, all Amritsar came out to pour their soul at his feet. The women of the Holy City of Song welcomed him with the Master's song, and went singing all the way with him to the village *Walla*, where he stayed in the lowly abode of a devoted disciple.

Tegh Bahadur could not stay in one place, for the accumulating sorrows of the people grew to be more than he could bear. He was perpetually on tour, meeting his disciples in villages and in lonely jungle-huts. He travelled as far as Dacca and Kamrup in Eastern India burning lamps of human hearts in memory of Guru Nanak, wherever the Master had been before him. At Dhubri, Tegh Bahadur raised a mound. He organized a Sangat in Assam, and illuminated many a family with the light of his face.

BIRTH OF GOBIND RAI

During his travels towards the East, in which his mother and his wife accompanied him, his son Gobind was born. Tegh Bahadur had to leave his wife at Patna when he went to Assam. Gobind, the Bala Pritam, the Child-

Beloved, was born at Patna in the absence of his father. When the latter returned from his tour in Assam, he lived at Patna for some time; but left them again there, when he with his five disciples journeyed on to Anandpur in the Punjab. He did not wish the mother to travel till her baby had grown old enough to bear the journey to the Punjab. Tegh Bahadur was at Anandpur, and his family were at Patna, where Gobind spent his childhood and part of his boyhood. The parting from Tegh Bahadur was always poignant for his mother and wife, and now for his child also. "But such is the call of Heaven", he used to tell them as he left. As we see, after an unusually long absence they had met at Patna to be separated this time for many years.

Bala Pritam, the Child-Beloved

The irrepressible spirit of Gobind Singh as a boy are recorded by a true disciple of his in a book called *Bala Pritam*, recently published by the Khalsa Tract Society, Amritsar. It is the result of careful study of the Patna life of Gobind Singh which recalls the analogy of Krishna. At Patna he won all hearts, and became a new centre of Dhyanam for devotees to whom he was able to give the Divine Signs that characterize spiritual genius. He would appear as Rama or as Krishna in response to the wishes and visions of the people of Patna. In the bright disc of the morning sun, seated on the banks of the Ganges, the self-closed eyes of these devotees saw Gobind, the Beloved, standing in the sun and shooting golden arrows from his blue bow.

He used to play tricks upon Patna housewives and the maidens and to overcome them with mirth. Breaking and piercing their earthen pitchers with his arrows he diverted all and delighted himself. Mata Gujri, the grand-mother of Gobind Rai, gave them new pitchers every time.

Raja Fateh Chand Meni and his queen are childless. The disciple Pandit Shiv Dutt points out Gobind to their empty eyes. The King and the Queen think of the merry boy, and pray for a child. One day the boy goes stealthily to their palace, and sees the queen sitting in deep reverie with her eyes closed. He approaches her very quietly, and suddenly throws his little arms around her neck; and, as she opens softly her rapture-red eyes, he looks into them and says, "Mother !" The Gobind's one word "Mother" takes away all her lifelong grief. He fills her heart and that of Fateh Chand with himself. God comes to them as a child, for they want a child !

The whole of Patna was Gobind's. He was the shining spot where people saw God. Gladness came to them when they saw him, conversed with him, touched him, or were playfully teased by him. Gobind Rai displayed infinite mischievousness which, his mother and grandmother, interpreting it as a sign of coming greatness, ignored. Years afterwards when Bala Pritam was at Anandpur, his disciples of Patna went to him on a holy pilgrimage. The old frail frame of Shiv Dutt accompanied this caravan of disciples, led by Raja Fateh Chand and his queen. The Master came many miles to receive them. Still mischievous, he concealed himself and let the caravan pass; and then, getting behind the palanquins that bore Shiv Dutt, Raja Fateh Chand, and the queen, he startled them with his old Patna whoop; throwing them all into that kind of joyful confusion in which everyone ecstatically forgets himself. Thus did Bala Pritam meet his devotees again.

Tegh Bahadur had but a brief time at Anandpur, where his family from Patna had now joined him. Gobind was about eight years old. During this brief sojourn, he made Anandpur the city of the disciples. It was already their natural fortress when they needed shelter. The kings of the land were then the avowed enemy of the Sikh, who was compelled to be ever ready to lay down his life for the truth. The hymns of Tegh Bahadur were composed to infuse the spirit of fearlessness into disciples, as there were times coming when the Sikhs would be called on to embrace death as a bride. Guru Tegh Bahadur's resolve to die for the cause inspired every Sikh man, woman, and child, once more with willingness to die.

The emperor Aurangzeb had adopted a cruel policy of extermination against the Sikhs, whom he considered to be grave political danger to his centralized Empire. It is well known now how he persecuted the non-Moslem, constantly dreaming of a Moslem Empire In India. Had he succeeded, it would have been one of the greatest historical achievements for the Moslem, and the name of Aurangzeb would be one of the greatest. But he failed to massacre the non-Moslems in numbers sufficient for the attainment of his purpose.

However, the Hindu shrines were thrown down in cities like Benaras and Brindaban in broad daylight, and mosques raised instead. The official sword put to death all those who refused to accept Aurangzeb's political religion. Darkness of pain spread all over the country, and despair filled the house of the non-Moslem. Nothing was held sacred—mother, wife daughter, and cow of the non-Moslem, were considered the rightful property of the Mussalman. To kill a Hindu, "a Kafir" was represented as a religious duty. The Mohammedan law was interpreted to sanction the annihilation of those who refused the authority of Islam. The whole country rose, with one cry, one prayer, and one curse, against the blind tyranny. The Brahmans from Srinagar, Kashmir—the Guru's Kashmir—flocked to Anandpur, bewailing their lot in that high solitude of the Himalayas where the Moslem Governor had nothing but death and torture and shame for them. His fury knew no control and his tyranny no limit. The Master had heard the wail of the people long before they came but now the time had come when he must rise and sacrifice himself to make the people free.

On the day when he was to give his decision, his young son Gobind Rai approached him and enquired, "O Father ! why are you so silent today ?" He replied, "You know not my child, the state of the people. Their rulers are as wolves, and there is no end to their misery and shame." "But what is the remedy, father ?" said the child. "The only remedy, my child, is to offer a God's man as an oblation in this fire; then the people will be secured from this misery," said the father.

"Offer thyself, father, and save the people," said Gobind Rai. The child was right, there was nothing else to do; the Master must sacrifice himself for the people, the son of God must be bled to pour life into the people—such is the ancient mystic law of life.

The Master was again obliged to take leave of his beloved son, his mother, and his disciples; and this time his journey was to a destination whence he would not return to them in that familiar physical shape. The city of Anandpur was by this time all put in order. There was the Master's botanical garden, a never-failing fountain, the academy of disciples, the temple of his praise, where gathered his disciples from far and near, with that joyous hilarity of soul, which was found nowhere else but at his feet. Gobind Rai was to be the Tenth Master as was universally known. The steel of ages past and ages to come shone with blue glint in the aura of the child Gobind. The Dhyanee eyes saw him even as a child, touching heaven with the crest of his turban. He was the Talisman of eternity, that could melt sun and moon and infuse the light into men's hearts.

Even in the presence of Tegh Bahadur, Anandpur shone with Gobind, who had already learnt the arts of archery, sword-playing, and horsemanship. He had learnt how to make poems, at the feet of his father; there were gathered at Anandpur all kinds of experts to equip him with the best possible training in the arts of life. This time it was not the disciple Gobind that had to part from the Master, as it was in the case of the disciples Lehna, Amardas, and Ram Das; it was the Master that was to go from his disciple. The disciple, Gobind already initiated by the Master into the perfection of Guru Nanak's Dhyanam, and to remain at Anandpur, and the Master had to tear himself away from the Beloved.

The emissaries of Aurangzeb came to Anandpur to summon the Master to Delhi; but he would not go with them, he promised to follow. He had yet to go to see disciples who were thirsting for him, those that lived on his way to Delhi. He took his own time and his own road; it lay through the midst of his disciples, and it lay covered with their flower-offerings. At Agra the Master with five chosen disciples delivered himself to the Emperor's men there awaiting him—he had taken so long in coming that they doubted his promise. He was then taken to Delhi.

The Master was kept in prison at Delhi and tortured there, under the orders of Aurangzeb. But all torture was to him as a mud spray against a mountain wall. Like Arjun Dev, Tegh Bahadur never for a moment took his mind out of the Dhyanam of Reality. Not a thought of curse or retaliation disturbed his peace, not a frown wrinkled his shining brow. As calm as at Anandpur, he maintained a peace of mind that the dissolution of three worlds could not have disturbed. Bhai Mati Das, seeing him in prison, felt deeply agitated, and said, "O Master, permit me to go. I will immediately make the ramparts of Delhi strike against the ramparts of Lahore, in a thunder-stroke, reducing all this Empire to thin powder. Allow me, I will crumble these tyrants like clods of clay in my hand." "O brother," said the Guru, "this is true; but ours is to think of Him. Ours is to live in His will and to be happy in seeing it work. Ours is not to plan out our own defence, seeing that the Beloved receives our injuries in his own heart." Bhai Mati Das fell speechless at the Master's feet. Truly the essence of real power is to live in the supreme peace, come death or torture. The great never complain.

The Master was asked to accept Aurangzeb's political religion, or to die. He chose death. Bhai Mati Das was sawn across at Delhi as if he had been a log of wood. The saw was made to run through his body as he stood erect. The more they pierced Bhai Mati Das with it, the deeper resounded from his flesh the song of Nam; for, after his agitation, he had been embraced by the Guru and thus put in the centre where there is no pain. The other Sikhs left for Anandpur with his messages, his poems, and the offerings of a cocoanut and five pice to Gobind Guru.

Tegh Bahadur was beheaded in Delhi, as he sat under the banyan tree reciting Japji. That banyan tree still stands. The Emperor Aurangzeb had insisted on seeing some miracle of the Master. "Cut off my head with your sword and it will not be cut," so had said the Master. A great dust storm swept that day over Delhi, and the sky was blood-red. This storm of dust carried off the Empire of Aurangzeb as if it were a dead leaf lying on the road. The Master yet lived.

X

THE TENTH MASTER
GOBIND SINGH NANAK

ANANDPUR OF THE TENTH MASTER

Out of the joy of the Masters have grown the names of our cities, filtering down into the common language of the people ! The Sikhs gave to the Punjab thirty-five new words for "Joy". Guru Nanak founded, on the Ravi, the city of the Creator—"Kartarpur". "Goindwal" is "The city of God". Amritsar means the "pond of Ambrosia", or "Lake of Immortality". Guranditta, son of the Sixth Master, named Kiratpur "city of praise". Anandpur is "the city of divine bliss", founded by Tegh Bahadur. At the martyrdom of Tegh Bahadur there was no sorrow at Anandpur; the new Nanak, Gobind, led the town in celebrating the event with a new purity of joy.

"Tegh Bahadur is gone !
The world says, 'Alas ! Alas !'
The heaven rings with hallelujahs !
Welcoming his return home !
The angels sing 'the victor comes home ! the victor comes home !'
All victory is in the Dhyan of His Glorious Name !
His disciples and his saints sit still in His supreme Dhyanam !
And in His love is freedom for them !"

Anandpur was made once again, under the divine

leadership of Gobind Singh, the City of Immortal Bliss.
Nothing was lacking, the former Master had provided
everything for his children. He gave all his soul to his
people, coming no more in earthly form to them. He knew
it; though they did not and could not know of his purpose.

Gobind Singh, too, brought new delight to the Sikh
people. He scattered joy and light in an abundance hitherto
unknown even in the Sikh life of the past nine generations
of this dispensation of divine grace !

Anandpur was a centre of life of the people : spiritual,
mental and physical. Around the Master assembled poets
and painters, and scholars; and he encouraged the devel-
opment of art and learning in his people. The disciples were
sent to Benaras to learn Sanskrit. He caused many long
Sanskrit books to be translated into Hindi. In fact, the
disciples had returned to their own line of work, forgetful
of the injuries inflicted on them by the kings. There was a
tremendous revival of literature and art at Anandpur. We
have accounts of this period from the Dhyanam of Bhai Vir
Singhji, in the little brochures published by the Khalsa Tract
Society, Amritsar. One of these, *Malin, or the Gardener's
Wife*, lifts up the curtain that time had let fall on Anandpur,
and allows us to see more of that place and its society than
is permitted by any earlier historian.

MALIN, OR THE GARDENER'S WIFE

Mohina and Sohina were once rich people but they had
renounced all in love of Nanak. They were accomplished
singers, gardeners, flower-breeders and poets. They came
in disguise as poor people, and entered Gobind's service in
his garden. They never tried to see him as they had once
had a sentence pronounced against them by a Sikh—"He
will not grant you a glimpse of himself" : these words had
escaped the lips of the Sikh when he was fatally wounded
and dying of thirst, and when he was refused water by
Mohina and Sohina who were carrying sacred water to the

temple for the worship of their stone deity—for at that time they were idol-worshippers. They had been so haunted by the face of the Sikh that they had returned hurriedly from the sanctuary to give him the very same water, but the Sikh had died meanwhile. His voice rang in their empty souls, "He will not grant you even a glimpse of himself." One day Kesara Singh (*Saffron Singh*), the Guru's gardener, exhibited specimens of their work of plant-breeding and making many a flower bloom out of its season, and named them to the Guru. Nobody else knew anything about them. He looked up to the sky, and repeated in an undertone the words of the dying Sikh. "He will not grant you a glimpse of himself." Then he added, "Tell them they cannot see the Master yet." But the Mother afterwards paid them occasional visits in their neat nest-like hut in the garden, and they used to sing the song of the Master to her. Every morning, whatever the season, they sent her a garland of flowers, with which the Mother garlanded the Beloved. One day, a Faqir called Roda Jalali came and begged of the couple for some of their flowers that seemed to him a curiosity at that season. Mohina and Sohina could not part with them; they were sacred. Roda Jalali stole like a cat into the garden at night, and plucked all the flowers with a view to presenting them to the Guru in the morning. Next morning, as the Master was sitting in the assembly of disciples, Roda Jalali presented himself and made an offfering of the basket of flowers. "Why did you not bring Gold Mohurs as an offering ?" said the Master. "Faqirs never touch gold," said Jalali. "Then a Faqir should come empty handed," said he, "the empty hands of a Faqir are beautiful." "But one must come with an offering," said Jalali. Thereupon the Master made a sign to Bhai Mani Singh to take off Roda Jalali's cap from behind—when lo ! a few gold Mohurs fell out of it. Meanwhile the Guru, looking at the flowers, cried like a grieved father, "O Roda ! you have not plucked flowers from the bush, but you have torn two souls from God." Saying this, the Master ran barefooted to the hut of Sohina and Mohina. The couple had already fainted amid their despoiled bushes, they seemed near to death. He revived them with his glance, and sat by them, lifting their heads into his lap while the Mother gave them water to drink. Their opening eyes saw those of the Master gazing deeply into them. Thus did Mohina and Sohina enter the path of discipleship.

BHAI NANDLAL AND GHYASSUDDIN AT ANANDPUR

Bhai Nandlal had migrated from Kabul to India with his wife and children. Providing them with a house at Multan, Bhai Nandlal entered the imperial service at Agra, becoming Secretary to Bahadur Shah, the son of Aurangzeb. He was a poet, and an Arabic and Persian scholar and he solved many a knotty theological problem in the theology of Al Quran, which were referred to him by the Prince. Once, when every other scholar had failed to satisfy Aurangzeb as to a particular verse in the Quran, Bhai Nandlal's exposition, given to the Prince in private, when repeated to the Emperor, gave him great pleasure. Thus was the scholarship of Bhai Nandlal brought to the notice of the Emperor, who ordered that so able a person should no longer be allowed to remain a Hindu. The news leaked out; and Bhai Nandlal saw that, to avoid death or apostasy, he must flee. He thought of escaping with his devoted Faqir-follower Ghyassuddin to Anandpur, and taking shelter with the Tenth Master. So with a few valuables they escaped by night from Agra, on two mules. When they reached Anandpur, they saw Gobind Singh sitting in the midst of a happy congregation. Bhai Nandlal and Ghyassuddin offered their homage and took their seats, as the Guru blessed them and welcomed them. Addressing Ghyassuddin, Gobind said, "Brother Ghyassuddin, to whom dost thou belong?" Ghyassuddin pointed to Bhai Nandlal, and said, "To him, Sire!" At this, one of the disciples wished to correct him; but the Master promptly

stopped him, saying, "There is no dispute at all. Brother
Nandlal belongs to me, and brother Ghyassuddin belongs
to Nandlal; so, O good man ! both belong to me." These
words were enough for Bhai Nandlal; he was thenceforward eternally his. By these words, and in these words, the
Master gave the gift of Nam to both, and they entered the
path of discipleship.

Bhai Nandlal, once he had laid his head at his Master's
feet, never left his presence. The Master was overwhelm-
ingly kind to him, and always addressed him affectionately
as "Nand Lala"—Master of joy. He would compose Persian
verses in praise of the Guru, and recite them everyday. We
have two volumes of these Persian poems.

GOBIND SINGH IN DISGUISE

Gobind Singh often sported with his disciples and had
many surprises for them. It was ordained at Anandpur that
every disciple should keep a *langar* of his own to feed the
pilgrims and passers-by, and the orders were that none
should be sent away disappointed. Very early one day, the
Master disguised as a common pilgrim, went round all
these *langars*, asking for bread. The disciples were busy
getting the bread ready, so they could not promise
anything till they were fully prepared to receive guests. The
Master went from door to door, till he reached Bhai
Nandlal's *langar*. Bhai Nandlal welcomed the guest with a
beaming face and brought everything that was in the room :
butter, half-kneaded flour, half-cooked pulse, and other
vegetables, and placed before the guest. "This is ready and
is all for you, but if you permit me, I will prepare them for
you, and serve you in the Name of My Master," said Bhai
Nandlal. Next morning, the Guru told everyone that there
was but one Temple of Bread at Anandpur, and that was
Bhai Nandlal's.

GOBIND SINGH AND "RENUNCIATION OF THE SANYASI"

A group of Hindu Sanyasis came to Anandpur, and complained to the Master that he was not laying sufficient emphasis on the virtue of Renunciation. He replied, "My disciples are men of renunciation in joy; their bliss is infinite, and no more is needed; all things come to their hands, and they use them as they need. As long as they do not go under illusion (Maya), so long they are free and pure. If one has obtained Self-Realization, of what use, my friends, is Renunciation ?" They were for arguing further, when he interrupted them, playfully bidding his Sikhs to put live charcoal on the lids of their Cocoanut Bowls of Renunciation. And as the lac cementing the joints melted off under fire, the bowls were shaken and gold Mohurs dropped out giving an open proof of their hypocrisy.

The scenes of Gobind Singh's life at Anandpur are lit by laughter, and joy. He would welcome his disciples with a smile or a touch on the shoulder, and he delighted in surprising them by his play of wit. Anandpur was alive with continual festival : "Every day a new year's day, and every night a wedding night" !

Gobind Singh is Guru Nanak; but he rides a splendid steed, arms himself with a quiver full of arrows and a mighty bow, has a sword hanging in his belt and a hawk perched on his hand and eyes that sparkle with joy and valour of the soul. His heart is gay because of his uncontainable joy.

THE ANCESTOR OF THE PUNJAB KALALS

There came into the assembly a Kalal, or wine distiller of the Punjab, a member of the most-hated caste. (It is said that the punishment for merely stepping on the bone of a *Kalal* is seven generations in hell. The hatred was of the caste-hatred type; and not hatred for the wine he made, for the Kshatriyas and other castes consumed wine freely even in the Mahabharata times). He stood at a little distance. The

Master invited him to come and sit in the assembly on which he hesitated and said that he was a *Kalal*. The Master immediately answered, "No, come in; you are not a *Kalal* but *Guru Ka Lal*," a ruby of the Master. Such was Gobind's attitude towards the low castes, and submerged humanity : he loved to lift them, and he did it by his looks. He raised them to the dignity of his own children by his baptism of love. His transmuting touch was the secret.

The Master had called for a cup of water, which was brought to him by a nobleman's son, a handsome young man with clean white hands. The water was crystal clear, and the cup scrupulously clean; but the Master after taking it in his hand, returned it to the young man without drinking, and said, "My son, it seems your hands have not yet laboured in the service of the saints." "No, sir, I have never worked with these hands yet," said the boy. "Ah ! My boy, go and make them pure first in the service of the saints."

Anandpur was the centre where all castes and creeds and colours met in one joyous crowd; as formerly they met at Kartarpur, Goindwal and Amritsar. Hundreds of thousands jostled to catch a glimpse of the Master.

The Master pondered deeply on the destiny of these people; for this was the last incarnation of Guru Nanak, as he alone knew. What was to become of them ?

Henceforth the disciple must be made the vehicle of the spirit of Guru Nanak, with the Word of the Master enshrined in his heart, as the Deity of this Temple. Henceforth they who would thirst for his Presence, must kiss his feet and his body by taking the Word into their souls.

THE CALL OF THE MASTER

Gobind Singh fixed a day for the gathering of all his disciples at Anandpur. When they had gathered from all parts of the country, he rose with the naked steel in his hand and called for a life to be offered to his steel from among their number, if they wished to continue as his disciples. This call caused some terror in the assembly; for they had already forgotten the ways of Guru Nanak, and that this was not the first time in Sikh history that some such call had been made. Guru Nanak had called in the same awful tone, and only Angad had come forward—the others being afraid. Moreover, the disciples knew their present Master only in his loving and sustaining mood; and, as they failed at the time of Guru Nanak, it is not surprising that now they were unable even to guess the meaning of the Master, for whom this was a climacteric moment in which centuries throbbed to new life. The Master called again, "Does any disciple wish to die under my steel ?" Only one rose and came forward with his head bent in deep reverence, saying, "Thine it is for ever, Master; under the keen edge of thy steel is the highest bliss." A tent was pitched on a little mound nearby, and the blessed disciple followed the Master into the tent.

The Master came out again with his flashing sword, saying, "One more disciple to die today !" So did he call five times in all and five Sikhs stepped forward to die.

After a while, out of the tent came the *Beloved Five*, decked in saffron-dyed garments and saffron turbans; altogether a new type, with the Master in their midst looking strangely as one of them. The *Beloved Five* by his favour had the same dress, the same physical appearance, and the same Divine glow, as he. Gobind Rai proceeded to dissolve the song of the Master (God word) in water; and he prepared the Nectar of Knowledge Absolute in the immortal draught in which he had resolved to give himself away to the children of Guru Nanak !

The Nectar was ready as he had just finished the chanting of his Mantram, when the Mother of his disciples came with sugar-crystals and stood waiting before the Master. "Welcome, good lady !" said he, "power without the sweetness of soul means little. Pour the gift into the Nectar, so that our disciples may be blessed not only with power but with the grace of a woman-sweet soul." And the Mother thereupon sweetened the Nectar.

The Blessed Five were as fully-armed soldiers in appearance, with the tresses of each tied in a *knot of disciple Dharma* gathered on the crown of the head and covered by a graceful turban; and they wore a kind of half-trousers. From within the Master's tent came out a new incarnation of the disciple, a new face of the Saint-soldier who had accepted death in love. It was a moment of creation whose full fruition requires the lapse of aeons.

He stood up, with the sacred Nectar contained in a steel vessel, to give the blessed abundance of *God-in-Man* away. The disciple from Bir-Asan, kneeling on his left knee, looked up to the Master to receive his eternal light. The Master gazed into the eyes of the disciple, and showered on his face the Nectar, calling him aloud with each shower to sing the Mantram composed by the Master for the occasion : "Wah-Guru Ji Ka Khalsa, Sri Wah-Guru Ji Ki Fateh." *The Chosen Ones, the King's servants, the disciples, the Khalsa, belong to the Glorious Master, all triumph be to His name ! He is Truth, and Truth triumphs now.*" He did it three times. The knot of Disciple-Dharma, which the Master had just gathered in his own hand, was then anointed by him with the same Nectar. Thenceforward every hair of the disciple's head was filled with his Nectar; every hair was a tongue which was to sing the Song of the Master. Every hair of the disciple is thus sacred for all time. Thus were the Five Beloveds anointed by the Master, and they were asked to drink the Nectar from the same steel cup in deep draughts of brotherly love.

"You are the Sons of Nanak, the Creator's own, the chosen ones.

I name ye the Khalsa.

Ye are the disciples of Song, and ye shall be the saviours of man.

Ye shall own no property, but all shall be for the Master.

Ye shall love man as man, making no distinction of
     caste or creed.

Ye shall keep for ever this flame of life lit in you,
     unflickering, in deep meditation on the One Death-
     less Being.

Ye shall bow your heads down to your Master only.

Ye shall never worship stock, stone, idol or tomb.

Ye shall always pray in the Dhyanam of your Master.

Remember always in times of danger or difficulty the
     Holy Names of the Masters, Nanak, Angad, Amardas,
     Ramdas, Arjun Dev, Har Gobind Sahib, Har Rai
     Sahib, Har Krishan, Tegh Bahadur.

I make ye a Rosary of these names; and ye shall not pray
     each for himself, but all for the whole Khalsa.

In each of you the whole brotherhood shall be incar-
     nated.

Ye are my sons, both in flesh and in spirit."

THE DISCIPLES BAPTISE THE MASTER

After this, Gobind Singh asked his Five Beloved
Disciples to prepare again the Nectar as he had prepared
it, and to anoint others with it as he had done. The Five sat
in a group, and, inspired by the Master, prepared the
Nectar in the same way. It was the Master himself who
offered first of all to drink the Amritam from the hands of
the Beloved Five. From Guru Gobind Rai his name was
changed to Guru Gobind Singh. Thereupon, the whole
heavens resounded with the joyous ejaculation, "Sat Sri
Akal"—"the only Reality is He"—the deathless, the timeless
Glory ? Thousands of Sikhs were anointed on that day with
the sacred Word—Amritam of the Master. It was this
Amritam that changed the docile, poor, fearful disciples
into the leonine name of the new Khalsa : Saint-soldiers,
who were taught to salute the God and the Master with a
naked sword swung high in air, and to practise the Simran
of Mantram of Wah-Guru. Arms were thenceforward the

symbol of a disciple's fervour of soul.

This great miracle of creation, done by Gobind Singh, transmuted Anandpur into the centre of a new Saviour-Nation. A contagious spirit of independence arose and spread, and the face of the country changed. Where love is supreme, the heart in which it resides must be clothed in splendour of steel; the flashing sword of love must be the expression, in this dark world, of the light of soul. "I am thine, death is nothing to me. I wear arms, not to kill, but to dazzle with their flash the eyes of cowardly kings, and to blazon in letters of fire, supreme majesty of love over all. I need no kingdoms on this earth; I lust not for shining gold, nor for the beauty of woman. I own nothing. All belongs to Him, the Lord ! If he has chosen to adorn my smile of Knowledge Absolute with the flash of His cleaving sword, it is his pleasure. My Religion then is of His Sword.

"Do not misunderstand me. I know the truth, I am made of it, I am in the safe-keeping of the Beloved. His pleasure is my salvation. I have no need to act, for all action has ended for me in His love. But so He wills; and I take the body of flesh to the altar of sacrifice for the sake of suffering humanity, and, rising out of the Master's heart still half-asleep, I go forward and die for others. With my blood, I will buy them in this world of trade and money-getting, a moral and physical relief. I covet no more but to die naming Him, with His song on my lips and his Nectar flowing out of my mind; fixed on the one purpose, to die for others and to save them from misery ! I therefore pray I may die, not in solitude, but in the battlefield; and not for my glory, but for the glory of one Song that is deathless."

AKALI

The human spirit at Anandpur manifested its joyous spiritual energy in many ways. On everyday that dawned there were new ideas in the very air, and the Khalsa crystallized in many shapes. The Sevapanthis, the Nirmalas, the Sahej-Dharis, set forth new shining resolutions; and, last but not least, came the Akali, who washed himself clean of all earth and earthly life, till absolutely free from the illusion of flesh and immersed in the vision of the Guru. Sevapanthis reserved themselves for the creed of service; later on they formed the first "Red Cross" corps of Gobind Singh, serving friend and foe alike. They carried water on their backs in the battlefield, and held the bowl of mercy to the thirsty lips of the dying. They carried a stock of first aid, and gained special knowledge in surgery and medicine. Nirmalas devoted themselves to learning. They studied Sanskrit and Vedanta, and went about educating the country and spreading the literature that took its rise in Anandpur. Sahej-Dharis, "*Disciples of the vow of moral devotion,*" was a beautiful name given to the disciples who could not yet stand up to wear the sword of the Khalsa, since wearing the sword meant death and dissolution. They would rather be in the background, the sympathizers, the hidden disciples of the Master. "They also serve who only stand and wait."

The Akali was the Khalsa with an increased share of the Master's Amritam in him. He was already immortal; he had shaken off his body; there was no consciousness in him of death, sin, or self. He recked nothing, he heeded nothing. So great was the power of soul in him that he called Death—"*ascension to Heaven (Charahi).*" If he ate raw "grams" he said he was having a "meal of almonds." He called the silver and the gold coins "husks," "pieces of broken china." His arithmetic began with Sawa Lakh (1,25,000). Whenever an Akali entered the city, he said, "The Armies of the Khalsa have arrived"—he never said "I". When anyone asked, "how many ? he said, "*Sawa Lakh.*" Whenever he wanted anything he did not "beg", but he said that he had only come to collect "taxes of the Khalsa."

Some ill-informed writers have depicted the Akali as a kind of human wild boar, because he was sincere to the point of savagery. He was armed from head to foot, "covered with steel"; his flesh was steel, and his eyes shone with the blue fire of destruction if anyone touched him wrongly. But he was the disciple, full of the Nectar of the divine song. If they were to cut him, they would find nothing but *Hari Nam* in his blood and bone. Was it not a marvel that at the call of Gobind Singh, there came a kind of men who soon rid the country of its weakness and won a respect for the Master's personality that no king could command ? "Akali" means deathless or timeless. "Kill me, cut me to pieces, I never die. I am Akali, out of this Door I go, out of that door I come in again. His touch has emancipated me. I am knowledge absolute, I am purity absolute, I am love absolute."

The Akalis called Emperor Aurangzeb by the curtailed name of "Auranga"; their language turned the world's glories and greatnesses into objects of contempt. They acknowledged no kings, and perhaps that it is why no Akali could be tolerated in the British Punjab.

Without intending it, no doubt, the present rulers in India, in the ordinary course of their administration, have made the existence of the Akalis in the Punjab of today impossible. For an Akali would allow no laws to interfere with his indigo garments, his infinite self-confidence, his prophetic-like majesty and sincerity combined with the simplicity of a child in his love of his Master.

The creation of the Khalsa in India is the culmination of Guru Nanak's genius, and the written character of his Word. The Amritam of the Tenth Master completely transmuted the men drawn from low or high castes of India, drawn from the Hindus or the Musalmans. After the Amritam, the Khalsa resembles no parent type of his own. For making the universal nation of man—apart from the characteristics that delimit races and nations—for the evolution of one united family of men on earth, Gobind Singh had shown the way in his Khalsa which he brought out ready-made from his brain, as Jupiter brought out Minerva. In the Khalsa is his type of the universal "super man" dead drunk with the glories and powers of the Infinite, yet sweet as a woman, innocent as a child, the *Bhai* "brother," of all, "striking fear in naught nor himself afraid of aught." He has given to him also a form which the great Master dreamt for the future universal man of God belonging to no one country, caste or creed. In the Khalsa there is seen the blending of the whole spiritual character of the man of the past and the future; as if it were a new creation.

Anandpur of the Master : now the Anandpur of the Khalsa ! The Khalsa chanted the new life-mantrams with united voice that passed like a thunder rolling over the hills : "Sat Sri Akal."

The Khalsa chanted the Song of the sword composed by Gobind Singh for their daily invigoration. He is said to have composed this song in adoration of some old Hindu goddess; but he merely employed the words used in Sanskrit literature in praise of an old goddess, adapting them to the praise of Steel. In recent history, under the leadership of Bhai Ram Singh, and inspired by the same old life-mantram, "Wahi-Guru," there again rose in the Punjab the semblance of the old Khalsa : the Kukas, whom the last generation saw sitting crosslegged in the posture of Yoga meditation, chanting this Song of the Sword, and springing to and fro— still in their sitting posture, like birds—to the accompaniment of their cry : "Sat Sri Akal, Sat Sri Akal." The original of this at Anandpur may be imagined. Whoever went to Anandpur in those days saw a new world, as if the veil of sky had been lifted at one corner and the celestial life was in sight. For in truth no one could recognize those Figures of Light made by the Master as anything of this earth. Pilgrims, both Hindu and Mussalman, came in singing caravans from all parts of the country to the City of Joy, which resounded day and night with the music of Nam.

HANSA ENTERS THE PATH OF DISCIPLESHIP

The Brochure *Bakshind Mahram* (the Beloved that Forgives), of the Khalsa Tract Society, describes how Hansa (it gives no full names, only the brief ones that the Khalsa adopted), a religous teacher of the Jains, came to the Master seeking for the "hidden light" that illumines the path of life from within. Hansa was a Pandit, a great painter and a leading monk. He brought an offering of a Painting of the sunrise, for Gobind Singh. But the orders were that he should not have an audience of the Master. After a few days, the disciples that took an interest in him, set up his painting in such a place in the garden, that the Guru (who encouraged all kinds of fine art) might see it. Gobind Singh saw it, and said, "The painting is full of light, but the painter's heart is all dark. He is cruel, very cruel." Saying this, he went away and said nothing more, indicating thereby to his disciples that he could not grant an audience to Hansa. This remark from the Master astonished the disciple, who had thought well of Hansa. Meanwhile the disciples and Hansa had many discussions in the garden on grave points of philosophy, the Guru's coldness remaining unexplained. Then, one day a palanquin came to Anandpur, borne by the Guru's disciples and containing what was little more than a living skeleton—though not long ago a handsome young man. He was lying in a helpless condition in pursuance of his vow of 'self-purification' and the Guru had sent for him. This young man, now half dead with the performance of his vows, was once in the same convent with Hansa, as a Jain Brahmachari. Near the same convent, there was a young girl, almost a child, whose parents had presented her to the Jain Temple as an offering in charge of Jain nuns. She and the young man belonged to the same town, where they had played together from their childhood upwards. Both loved each other at an age when they hardly knew what love was; but their guardians had separated them, putting the boy in the temple and the girl in the convent. Hansa was in charge of the temple. For years the young people did not see each other; then, while gathering flowers in the forest, they met for a moment and conversed.

This was a great sin according to the rules of the convent and the nunnery. The girl was punished by having her eyes put out. The boy was sent to the hills for a prolonged penance, from which he was rescued by the disciples.

Hansa was responsible for all this. As to the girl only Hansa knew her whereabouts, and he was asked to bring her to Anandpur. After a long search, the blind girl was brought by him to Anandpur. By this time, the great love of the Master, and the nursing of the disciples had brought the young Jain Brahmachari to full health again. He was sitting in the assembly, and the music of praise was in full song as the blind girl entered. The Master looked at her, and she saw the Master. Gobind Singh blessed her and initiated her into the Raja Yoga of Nam. It is written that she recovered her sight and that her face shone with celestial light. The Master's joy was great, and he ordered that the nuptials of these two disciples be celebrated then and there. Great was the rejoicing of the disciples. Hansa was initiated the same day, and made a "Singh" of the true faith.

Gobind used to go on excursions to various parts of the hills. He was invited by the Rajah of Nahan to stay with him. The Master went and lived by the Jamuna, at a point where stands the temple of Paonta Sahib today—on the other side of the river, at this place, runs the ancient trunk road to Srinagar, marked by Asoka's famous pillar at Kalsi. He stayed with the Rajah for months, giving full training to his disciples in art of archery and musketry. From here the Master went to Dehra Dun, the residence of the late Ram Rai, to see his widow, Mai Punjab Kaur and to settle her affairs.

PADMA, DAUGHTER OF THE RAJAH OF NAHAN

There was a large gathering of the Hill Rajahs at Riwalsar, where they had invited the Master to see the floating island in the lake of Riwalsar. The Master went with his disciples. The Rajahs had come thither with their queens, each of whom had a private audience of the Master. Padma, the talented daughter of Rajah of Nahan, saw the Guru here, and entered the path of discipleship. Padma's devotion to the Guru took a fatal turn : her tender soul blended with the light she beheld, so that to be separated from it was death; yet Padma must go back to Nahan. The air was thick with rumours that the Hill Rajahs were being compelled by Aurangzeb to fight against the Guru and to annihilate the Khalsa; Padma had heard this from her father, and had already tried her best to avert the danger; but some of the Rajahs were too cowardly to stand against the prestige of Aurangzeb. Nahan was a small estate, and did not count for much. The Rajah of Bilaspur was already jealous of the Guru's rising power. Padma knew that a war was imminent between the treacherous hosts and the glorious guest of Riwalsar. Before she left, she prayed to the Master that she might not live to see this cruel war against him; and he told Padma's mother, the Rani of Nahan, that the remaining days of her illustrious daughter were few. So it happened. Padma died soon after he left Riwalsar, and never saw the cruel war waged by the Hill Rajahs against him.

THE HILL RAJAHS, THE TOOLS OF THE MOGHAL EMPIRE

Gobind Singh had come to know of the evil intentions of Aurangzeb and how he was now pitting the Hill Rajahs against him. But nothing would disturb the peace of the City of Joy. The Rajah of Assam, a disciple, came on a pilgrimage; and, amongst many other valuable offerings, he brought a trained elephant named Pershadi for the Master. This elephant had a white stripe from the tip of his trunk all along his back, right to the end of his tail; he was trained to hold a fan in his trunk and wave it, and to do a hundred other feats. The Rajah of Bilaspur, in whose territory lay the city of the Guru, asked him to lend this elephant, but he declined as the Master would not part with a gift brought with so much devotion.

The Khalsa used to go for fuel and grass into the State forests, and many a time there were small skirmishes with the hill men, but the Rajahs never thought of disturbing the Master at Anandpur. They had already tasted the steel of the Guru's disciples, and they thought it best to leave the Khalsa alone.

But then came an unexpected turn of trouble. The Hill Rajahs came with their combined armies to attack the Master when he was on holiday at Paonta, hoping to surprise him and to take him prisoner; and there was fought a most deadly battle between the Guru's chosen few and the Hill Rajahs. The latter were finally routed; but imperial hordes joined with him and there ensued many actions against the Guru, with a like result. Pir Buddhu Shah of Sadhaura came to fight on the Master's side, and in one of these battles many of his followers and two of his sons were killed. Pir Buddhu Shah was a great devotee of the young Guru and carried his glorious image in his inmost Dhyanam.

Said Khan Enters Discipleship

The Master now entrenched himself and his people at Anandpur, which was soon besieged by the combined forces. They were scattered many a time in nightly sallies but reinforcements poured in from Lahore and Sirhind, till Anandpur was blocked, and no provisions, could enter. Many strange things happened during the following months of siege. A new general named Said Khan, brother of the wife of Pir Buddhu Shah, fresh from Ghazni side, was ordered to take command of forces besieging Anandpur. He went to Sadhaura to see his sister; and he found her mourning the death of her two sons, fallen in the opposite cause. Pir Buddhu Shah having returned from the battle-field, Said Khan began a little altercation with him because of his faith in a Kafir. The discussion was brought to an end by Nasiran who, in the midst of her deep sorrow, saw in a trance, the veil of sky torn and in the celestial realms, her two sons—in full angelic effulgence of perfected souls, bringing her immediate peace. She had never seen Gobind Singh; but, in the same realm of trance, she saw the glorious Master on his fiery purple steed riding past her, blessing her and saying, "Daughter, fear not; do not mourn—thy great sons live in the Higher Realms." It was his hand that had torn the veil. On rising from the trance, Nasiran understood what had attracted her husband to the saint of Anandpur; she, too, felt the same attraction now, and agreed with her husband that nothing of his could be kept from the service of such a one. "We breathe for the Beloved, we shall willingly die a thousand times to have but one glimpse of Him." Said Khan was the holy transfiguration of his sister, and was greatly perplexed, being under orders to lead the army against the Guru. He left Sadhaura for Anandpur. Even after that initiation into the path of discipleship, Nasiran lived in intense Dhyanam of the Master; she saw him clearly in the fort of Anandpur. The war was raging outside; inside the disciples still raised the music of praise to Heaven, and the limpid current of Nam flooded their souls. Gobind Singh led this joy, fed it from his soul and Nasiran, lived not in her body now, but there at his feet. A day came when she saw him ride on his blue steed into the enemy's camp, right up to general Said Khan. She saw Said Khan lift his gun and aim it at him; but Nasiran standing before Said Khan, shook it, so that the bullet missed its mark. This occurred as she remained at home in her Dhyanam, while, at Anandpur, the Master had gone to Said Khan on horseback all alone, and saw Said Khan level his gun at him as he approached, and miss. By this time, the Guru stood close to him, and said, "Come, Said Khan, let us fight." Said Khan was fresh from Sadhaura, and Nasiran's face was before his eyes as he beheld the Guru. "What is all this mystery, Sire ? Explain to me," said Said Khan. "Bow the head to my stirrup," replied Gobind. As Said Khan placed his head at the foot of the Master he entered the path of discipleship, obtained the seed of Simran. This took place in much less time than it takes to think of it, and lo ! the Master was gone. Before one of the enemies could realize what had happened, the Master had returned to his fort. Said Khan told nobody what had happened; he threw away his sword, changed the dress, "became poor," and suddenly left the battlefield for a lonely cave near Kangra, wither the Master had ordered him to go, there to pass his days in Simran.

THE MASTER BESIEGED

Thereupon the disciples began to starve and with them starved their Master, his four sons, his wife, and his aged mother—not to mention his elephant Pershadi and his horses, which wasted away and died. The Master was for remaining in the fort to the last, but his disciples could not bear to see him starve—much less his four little ones. They even wished to compel him to leave Anandpur; but he sternly bade them to leave him to die with them—otherwise he would go, after he had, by written word, disavowed his Master's hold upon them. Forty disciples wrote in reply disowning his leadership, and left him. They went to their homes; but Sikh mothers and Sikh wives alike disclaimed them, and there was no welcome for them anywhere. Then they bitterly repented, and wished to return to the Beloved; but they could not reach Anandpur, besides, by this time he has gone from Anandpur. After they left, an offer was made by the invading force to let the Master and his followers go without any injury to their persons or property, on condition that they vacated the fort. The Guru could hardly believe in this overture; but, in the end, the fort was given up, valuable contents being thrown into the river Sutlej that then washed its walls. Some loads of manuscripts, the literary labour of years, were included in the property that was to accompany the party. They had not gone very far from the fort, however, when the enemy fell upon them.

Gujri, the mother of Gobind Singh, and her two grandsons, escaped with a small party; only a Brahman cook was left as their sole attendant who took them to his village.

The mother of the Khalsa fled in another direction, while the Guru with a few Sikhs made towards Ropar. The manuscripts were nearly all destroyed in this affray; only a few translations from Sanskrit books, which now form our *Dasam Granth*, could be saved.

During this flight the Master never allowed the current of Nam in his disciples to ebb; he watched, and saw that fear of death had no effect on it. While fleeing, the Khalsa held its daily *Divans* of His Praise, sang the Word of the Master, and constantly kept itself refreshed with song.

The Sweetness of Death

Chamkor (now in the Tehsil of Ropar, Punjab) had small fortress, which Gobind Singh occupied. He had then with him about forty disciples and his two elder sons Ajit Singh and Jujhar Singh—the former being fifteen years old, and the latter thirteen. But soon the Imperial army, which was in hot pursuit, besieged this fortress also, and there was no way out but to fight and die one by one. The disciples held the fortress a long time, baffling the calculation of the enemy, as the Master kept up an incessant shower of his gold-tipped arrows. The disciples one by one would sally out, waving their swords in the midst of the enemy, and die. Ajit Singh entreated his father to let him also go and die, as his brothers were dying before his eyes. "O father ! I feel an intense desire for this death, and the feeling rises supreme in my breast that I must go and fight and share this last honour with my brothers !" The father lovingly embraced the boy, decorated him with sword and shield, dressed him fully as a soldier, and kissed him. "Go, my child ! Akal Pursha so wills." Ajit Singh, rode a horse into the thick of the battle, and waving his sword and crying, "Sat Sri Akal, Sat Sri Akal," departed for the true

Kartarpur of Guru Nanak. Gobind Singh saw him go, closed his eyes in prayer and accompanied the soul of Ajit Singh for a little distance beyond death's door till the boy was among the celestials. As the father opened his eyes, he saw the little one Jujhar Singh standing before him with folded hands with the same entreaty on his lips. "Father, I, too, wish to go where my brother has gone." "You are too young to fight," said the father. "What is age, father ? Have I not drunk my mother's milk, and have I not tasted the sacred Amritam ? Bless me, father, and let me go." Gobind Singh took the little one in his lap, washed his face, dressed him in a beautiful velvet suit embroidered with gold and silver, put a small belt round his little waist, and gave him a miniatrure sword. He wound a turban on his head, decorated it with a little crest, and kissed him. "My child," said he, "We do not belong to this earth. Our ancestors live with the Akal Pursha. You are now going; go and wait for me there." The child had gone but a little distance when he returned and said he was feeling thirsty. Gobind Singh again said, "Go, my child ! There is no water for you on this earth. See yonder, there is the cup of Nectar for you where your brother lies." This child then, rode the way his brother had gone.

Two Pathans Help the Master

Last of all Gobind Singh had to quit the fortress of Chamkor, and under cover of night he went whither the road might take him. He had already fasted for days, and this journey on foot utterly exhausted him; so he laid his head on a clod of clay and slept in the open field, having previously plucked and eaten a leaf of *Akk* to sustain himself. As he rose a shepherd saw him, and, recognizing him, wished to raise a cry; but the Master, without hurting him more than was necessary, sealed his two lips with an arrow, and escaped. As he entered the next village. Machhiwara, he was recognized again by his old admirers,

Ghani Khan and Nabi Khan, the horse dealers. These faithful friends received him with great respect, and concealed him in their house—as the Imperial army was still in hot pursuit. He was by this time joined by some of his followers. When the house-search became imminent, Ghani Khan and Nabi Khan disguised him and his followers in indigo-dyed garments as Mussalman Faqirs—throwing their long tresses back—and carried him, thus disguised as *Uch Ka Pir*, through the camp to a more secure part of the country. The commander suspected and interrogated these two men closely; but they proved more than a match for him, and carried the Master safely across.

THE TWO PRINCES BETRAYED

The Brahman cook Gangu, who took Mata Gujri and her two grandsons—Fateh Singh and Zorawar Singh—to his village on their flight from Anandpur, turned traitor and handed them over to the Nawab of Sirhind. The grandmother was kept in a prison-cell separate from her infant charges. The little ones, pale and livid with many day's privation, were produced in the Nawab's court as Princes, with absurd theatricality. The Nawab made a speech, in which he asked them to embrace Aurangzebian Islam or die. In the former case, he promised them all kinds of honours and joys and riches and comforts. The pale faces of the two Princes blushed red at the insult offered. Fateh Singh, the elder, asked the younger to remain quiet when he himself replied, "We are sons of the Master, Gobind Singh, and grandsons of Tegh Bahadur. The joys of senses are for dogs and asses; sacred Death, good Death, for us." Day after day they were harassed with similar temptations in the court; the Nawab trying to be kind to them, if they would accept Islam. When nothing availed, and the little heroes stood firm as rock, the Nawab called two Pathan youths whose father had been killed in a battle by the arrows of the Guru, and wished to hand the two boys over to them for any vengeance they liked to wreak on them. But the Pathan youths declined to do any injury to the two infants, saying, "No, sir, we will fight the enemy in the battlefield; but will not, like cowards, slay these two innocents."

After many days, a cruel form of execution was devised by the Nawab. The wall of Sirhind was thrown down for about three yards, these young ones of the Master were made to stand a yard apart from each other, and the order was given to build the wall little by little on their tender limbs; repeating at every foot and half foot of construction, the same alternative—Death or Islam ? The Princes stood with their eyes turned upward, seeing their heavenly ancestors come to bear them away and remained calm and speechless until the cruel wall entirely covered them.

Mother Gujri expired in the prison on hearing of the tragic end of her two beloved grandsons. Gobind Singh heard of this heart-breaking tragedy as he was passing across the country near Sirhind. He closed his eyes, and sent to Heaven the prayer embodied in his famous hymn— *The Message of us, the Disciples, to the Beloved.*

> "Give him the Beloved, the news of us, the disciples
> Without Thee, the luxury of soft raiment and sweet rest
>   is, for us, all pain;
> And these high palaces creep toward us like snakes !
> The lips of the wine cup cut us like thin-edged poniards.
> And dry as dust this jug of wine when Thou art not with
>   us !
> The pallet made of pale straw is Heaven for us, if Thou
>   be there !
> Burnt be the high palaces if Thou be not there !"

THE FORTY MARTYRS

The forty deserters never saw the Master again; but they did resolutely fight with the enemy, breaking his march on the Guru. They all died in battle, but they succeeded in scattering the enemy forces. The Guru came on the scene, saw that this attack on the enemy was the performance of his old devotees, and went round lifting each of their dead bodies with fatherly affection, wiping their faces, and blessing them. Only one, Bhai Mahan Singh was yet alive, and the Guru took him in his lap and asked if he had any wish to be fulfilled, any prayers to offer for life or immortality. "No, father ! I have no wish. I only pray that forty of us may be forgiven, and the ties that were broken once may be reunited so that we may live at Thy Feet." The Master tore the document they had given him at Anandpur, and said, "Dhan Sikhi, Dhan Sikhi, Dhan Sikhi—*How great is the discipleship* !"

LOVE GATHERING AGAIN

During these vicissitudes, the Master halted once in the Lakhi jungle where the disciples gathered round him again in hundreds and thousands. There he composed a very pathetic song; which, even now, brings tears to the eyes of us, his poor disciples.

O ! When they heard the call of the Beloved;
They came crying to Him,
So will the scattered herd of buffaloes fly to the long-
    absent Master on hearing his voice, dropping the
    half-chewn grass from their mouths as they hasten
    back to him.

THE MYSTIC FIRE

Then he went on with the concourse of his singing disciples and halted at a place called Damdama. He was still dressed in the indigo-dyed garments. One day a fire was lit, and he tore his indigo garments into shreds and burnt them shred by shred in the fire. Thus was the Moghal Empire burnt by him shred by shred.

It was at Damdama that the Khalsa came together

again, and Anandpur was reproduced there. The mother of
the Khalsa joined the Master. When she arrived, he was
sitting in the full assembly of the disciples, who were
singing his immortal songs. Addressing him, she said :

"Where are my Four, Sire ? Where are my Four ?"

He replied :

"What of thy Four, O Mother ?
What of thy four ?
When lives the whole people, the Khalsa here ?
Gone, gone are thy Four
As sacrifice for the life of these millions more, all thy
   sons !
O Mother ! what if thy Four are gone ?"

Gobind Singh wrote here his famous epistle *Zafarnama*,
to Aurangzeb. He sent for the original copy of *Granth Sahib*
from Kartarpur on the river Beas, but the foolish people
there would not part with it; so the Master sat in Dhyanam
of the Word, and dictated the whole of it to Bhai Mani Singh
out of his vision, as did Arjun Dev dictate to Bhai Guru Das.
Granth Sahib had a second birth from the Master, Gobind
Singh; and it came out of his soul, as came his Khalsa. In
this copy of *Granth Sahib* he changed only one word.
Khulasa (Freed man) was dictated by the Tenth Guru as
Khalsa (the Kings' own). And there was slight variation of
one letter in reproducing the whole volume out of his
intense Dhyanam.

This is our Sacred Granth which occupies the Throne on
which sat Gobind Singh. It is another "*Angad*." The Tenth
Master thus ends in the First, Guru Nanak, again.

ABCHAL NAGAR

After a short stay here, Gobind Singh left for Deccan,
where he settled on the banks of the Godawari at a place
known as Nander. Soon a city sprang up round him, and
he called it Abchal Nagar, the City of the Eternal, that

Moves Not. The last days of his earthly life were spent here in all the wondrous glow of Nam-life, as it began at Anandpur; it had been kept undimmed during the disciples' passage through the hatred of the enemies. Anandpur was reproduced here in Deccan again.

The disciple Said Khan came all the way from Kangra hills to see the Master. One day, in the full assembly of the disciples, a messenger arrived from the Punjab to Said Khan. Said Khan opened the letter, and passed it on to the Master. It was from his sister, Nasiran; and it was a song, an epic telling how the Emperor's minions ransacked Sadhaura, treating the saint Buddhu Shah as a rebel.

Nasiran wrote :

"Today Shah Sahib is gone to the Heavenly land !
And it is now my turn. These eyes have not seen the Beloved yet, but they have drunk of his beauty in Dhyanam. There is no sorrow. It is the inner joy blossoming up in the fulness of a willing death ! The soldiers are making house-searches today. My turn comes today or tomorrow.

"Second day—Lo, good brother ! They have come. I have tied a white handkerchief on my head, and I have slung a kirpan in my belt. I am fully dressed as a true soldier-disciple. Thy sister Nasiran, the Guru's Nasiran, is glad to die such a death. Lo, Brother ! Farewell ! But we have already met in Him for ever."

This messenger had been a long way, searching for Said Khan in the Kangra hills; and then after a long and weary journey he found him at Nander—Abchal Nagar—sitting in the joy-illumined, the sacred Assembly, lit by the Master's face.

As the letter was read, the Master closed his eyes and blessed his daughter Nasiran.

THE WORD CROWNED

The day came when the Master sent for a cocoanut and five pice, and placing them as an offering before the *Granth*

Sahib, he said :

> "So does the Akal Pursha ordain,
> The Word is Master now—
> The song of Nam, the *Guru Granth*.
> All Khalsa should seek the Master in his Word,
> And bow to *Guru Granth* as my successor."

Fully attired as a soldier, he mounted his blue horse, and rode away and disappeared behind the Veil.

> Sat Sri Akal
> Sri Wah-i-Guru Ji Ka Khalsa
> Sri Wah-i-Guru Ji Ki Fateh

XI

GURU NANAK : GLIMPSES OF HIS ART AND THOUGHT

NANAK AND HIS POETRY

Guru Nanak is the World-Teacher. He is also the teacher of one single, poor man unknown to name or fame. With him thought begins anew. One with Truth, Nanak stands supreme, towering heaven high above his surroundings, centuries ahead of his age, and looking at regions of mind and soul beyond this planet. He stands in supreme solitude of thought and power. Before his presence, before his mind, all bow down their heads. He is the creator. "Whoso can come and sit before me on a carpet and say 'I' is my disciple !"

He allowed no traffic with falsehood or half-truth, or with any kind of superstition, or with hypocrisy. He spoke with the voice of the deliverer to the oppressors of the people, whether Hindu or Mussalman, whether prince or priest. He condemned the imposition on the people of Brahmnical hypocrisy and priest-craft. He would not submit to a wrong system of education. He found both the Hindu and the Mohammedan faithless, misreading everything to suit their evil selves; and the teachers and preachers of the land deceiving and cheating the people.

He found the Krishna-worshippers dancing in open air theatres in wild and sensual frenzy. "They dance, and as they kick, the dirt, the dust of the streets settle on their heads. Ah, this singing and dancing is illusion."

He saw the doings of the Jain with utter disgust; to him it was a limit of the degradation of the human mind in the name of the religion of non injury. The whole people were steeped in darkness. The soul of the people was dead. The immorality of the highest class was appalling; both the religion and the politics of the land were adapted to wolves, not men and women. Guru Nanak stood as one man against the hosts of darkness, unafraid of aught, blowing his horn of freedom, shaking all the old foundations of society. A new creation, a New Life ! Except one, there is no parallel in the Indian history to the awakening that took its birth in the mind of Guru Nanak.

The following passages, taken from the writings of Guru Nanak, tell of the demoralization he found in the society of his time :

"They devour men alive, and yet they go and bow down to God in Namaz !

They wear the sacred thread who kill animals with the butcher's knife.

And the Brahmans come to the houses of the slayers of beasts and blow their conches and beg bread !

And they, too, relish the butchery !

There is no Dharma in the country, there is no honour of blood or name.

They have the Tilak on their forehead, they wear an ochre coloured Dhoti; but the knife is hidden in their sleeves, and they let the blood of the people.

The Qazis wear blue robes of holiness, and receive the offerings of the people.

The Hindus share the loot, and worship their deities with the loot they have gotten.

They kill the innocent; they share the blood of the people they have half-killed.

And then they say, 'Do not touch us, we shall be defiled !'

They sit in a sacred square made of prescribed lines drawn by themselves, and say, 'None is allowed to touch us, for our food would be soiled.'

> They sit there, in their sanctified squares and forbid the touch of another's hand, when what they drink is the people's blood !
>
> They levy taxes on the sacred cow and the holy Brahman without a thought; and think of crossing the sea of sin by being kind to the cowdung !
>
> They have sandal-paste tilaks on their foreheads, and have Dhotis for covering their legs with piety, and in their hands they carry the rosaries, O God !
>
> But they eat the crumbs of the Malechhas, and in privacy read the Quran to please their Masters !"

A devout Sikh told me, "Had I not found Guru Nanak, I would have sought the refuge of Buddha." Another man told me, "Guru Nanak was a born Buddha." In fact, there is a profound resemblance between the two. "Om ! I take refuge in Buddha, I take refuge in Sangat, I take refuge in Truth." That is Buddha's Mantram. "Om ! I take refuge in the Guru. I take refuge in Truth;" is the Mantram of Guru Nanak. Buddha proclaimed a new civilization that took its birth in his mind. Guru Nanak too, bases his authority on none but himself. "So says Nanak, so says Nanak !" is the burden of his songs.

One day, they say, a huge and very hungry crowd gathered at Kartarpur. Guru Nanak asked Lehna to çlimb a thorny acacia and shake its branches. Lehna climbed the tree and the crowds stood below, and he shook the tree with joy as the Master had ordered. The sacred music of Nanak the Master, flowed in streams of song from the swaying branches of the Kikar, and all who heard were filled with the harmony. This Music of the Master, is it not written in our very souls !

Once, we are told, when Lehna and Nanak were alone, Lehna saw that the feet of the Master as he lay asleep were being pricked as if by thorns. Lehna was astonished; because the Master was apparently fast asleep, and Lehna was sitting by his side. But a shepherd who was a disciple, was passing through thorn bushes with his sheep, and was in deep communion with Nanak, so that the shepherd's wounds from the thorns appeared on the feet of the Master. This too, is one of the parables that we treasure in our hearts.

Wherever he went, the hearts of the people were gladdened, and they began singing his Song of Silence, which is not written on paper, but on the hearts of his disciples; and there it still sings as of old.

Every disciple whom he chiselled in the image figure of "Dhyani Nanak" was a poem of his. The whole of his poetry, written in the soul to the longings of the people for freedom, for peace, was too deeply personal to be recorded on any printed page. Minds like Guru Nanak's are lost in the beauty of Thought, Vision and Prophecy. Their very looks write letters on the dust of the earth, their silence singing, enters the hearts of the people and searches the inmost soul. Some write poems, some sing poems, but Guru Nanak made poets by his touch. When he touched the forehead of a disciple and gave *him* peace, he threw the creative spark which sets fire to the heart and the singing flame of beauty sprang into the void.

Many of my Sikh sisters, who lost their husbands in the prime of life, have told me that they have found in Nanak's songs, more than all the world could give them. And I have sat at their feet and seen that the touch of their holy feet gave me peace of soul that I, poor gambler that I am, had lost for days. Whenever God grows less in me, I go and see them and find that they fill me with music.

In all lyric poetry there is a spirit of desire, and a secret *thirst*. The highest song is full of the *thirst for the divine*. It is all a longing and a desire. But there is no pain in the songs of Nanak. It is sung to fill his disciples with the peace of God, when they are faint and exhausted. It is the living fountain where hundreds quench their thirst. Nanak pours the infinite of his soul into his song; which is thence poured into the hearts of his disciples, which shares in the infinite.

The elements danced before Nanak and million-throated nature took up his hymns. The five rivers of the Punjab stil' sing his songs. The sky was his salver; the stars burnt as little lamps in his Temple.

There is a fragrance of roses as we name Nanak. While writing about him I have felt the shower of rose petals on these pages and the perfume of the Golden Temple all about me. When I was sitting in my room, miles away from the country of roses, and when the season of flowers passed, their fragrance was still there. Name "Nanak" and the Mystics Rose returns.

JAPJI

The hymn Japji is the burden of the whole *Guru Granth*.

The day of the disciples begins with *Japji*. The melody breaks forth in our inner ears with the strain of the "First dawn of Creation." Our eyes close, and as if in a dream, we stand listening to the music that rings through eternity.

We are the children of *Japji*. Its music is our motherland. It comes to us with an intimacy as close as if it were born of the hidden seat within our soul.

The maker of this hymn is so filled with its beauty, that he himself, the Master of its Music, is entranced with it.

Ever since its birth, every morning, in its chant we have the mingling of a myriad holy voices, the voices of the Disciples.

I feel at times that with *Japji* I am as one transported to the Land of Immortals. I am as one apart from the body, listening in wonder to a Voice reciting *Japji*.

In my reverie, I feel the singer has hands that touch my soul. Then I realize that *Japji* is the Word. With such visions, I do not feel lonely.

As we rise on the rhythm of *Japji*, where is distress or dust ? We transcend the tiny speck of the visible present. We are more than men we ever were. The sacred rivers roll down through the soul of man in the music of Guru Nanak's Dream. The trees arise as in prayer. The stars beam on the Dome of *Japji*, at another time they bejewel the minaret on the Palace of the King. The Sun and the Moon revolve around that Dome. Every speck of dust flies as a particle of gold, to write the Master's Name in *Japji*. At its sound, we hear the dance of feet on the grassy meadows around us; and in our reverie we see no flowers in the fields but have dropped from the breeze-blown, flying shawls of the mystic dancers.

The wheel of Karma rolls on, and man unaided cannot gain his freedom. But we rejoice when Japji tell us :

"The Heaven shall cover our shame with honour.
By our own deeds, we have made this tabernacle,
And by the light of His Glance we shall attain our
    Eternity."

Beyond *Nirvana*, *Japji* lights up for us the still Higher Realm of Mercy (*Fazal*) as the highest and the truest hope for man. It is beyond the physical, the *Karam Khetra* or the Realm of Action. It is beyond the Realm of Knowledge. It is deeper that the *Realm of Ecstasy*. Deeper than Ecstasy is *His Grace* and deeper still than the Realm of His Grace is *the Abode of God in us*. The Master's Song goes from the old to the new. It rises higher and higher; till the soul passes into the heavenly region where there is no speech or knowledge but the Infinite reposes in the Infinite.

"Endless is thy Creation,
We see nor Thy Near nor Thy far,
Thou hast nor this nor that shore,
We cannot touch Thy limits at any point."
"Salute the Beginning-less Beginning,
The colourless Purity,
The Deathless Verity,
The changing Permanence that changeth not through
    ages and ages."
"They say this Earth is borne on the Horns of the Bull.
    But there is Earth beyond earth, there are planets and
    planets beyond;
'Heavy indeed,' it is said, 'is the load on the Horns of
    the Bull !'

But it is not the Bull—it is *Dharma,* born of the Heavenly
Love that bears the weight of Worlds."

When the world beats us and breaks us by the weight
of its matter, we go to *Japji.* The sore melancholy of our
heart and mind is made whole by *Japji.* The soot on our
faces burns up, and they begin to glow like the burning roses.

In Guru Nanak's poetry is a marvellous devotion to "the
Infinite Being from which all comes, to which all goes." His
poetry affirms nothing as to the mere idea of this Being, but
is absolute in personal devotion to "The Beloved," and full
of the perpetual music of His Praise. "As the fish knows not
the nature of ocean, how wide and how vast, I know Thee
not; but I touch Thee, I live in Thee, and I die if I am taken
out of Thee."

To make the Universal will as our personal will, with all the
joys and delicious pain of human love is his intense passion.

His one song *Japji* marks him a Creator whose genius
puts its seal on the ages. The simple architecture of the song
is like that of the rock-hewn temples. They are the final
forms of his ideas in the language he has chosen to
speak. And he has rightly chosen to speak in his own
mother tongue. Every particle of its marble-cut Word-
Temple contains the design of the whole.

The language of *Japji,* though the common dialect of the
people, has been raised by the Master to a new power,
charged with the meanings he gave to it.

A HYMN OF NANAK

Thought is a miracle, what we see and hear is a miracle,
And love of knowledge, and peace of mind !
It is a miracle that we love one another,
Wind and water, fire and dust, are a miracle.
O Mother ! The arrow of His Kind Glance has wounded
me !
But none sees my pain
Nor do I know more than my own pain.

My mind is a Temple of love,
My body a robe divine,
The sacred Nectar flows in the Temple.
The Word is my breath, and the Song is my blood !
Beloved, think of me !
O ! The Unsensed, the Unknown that is visible and
 invisible !
Thou that art everywhere in every throb of life !
All temples of flesh are thine and under Thy shade,
Thou informest and inspirest and teachest,
I know no other but Thee,
I sing of Thee, as in me Thou sittest and singest.
O Love ! Thy seat is Eternity and great is Thy Name and
 Thy Glory.
Thou art Truth and Thou art Justice !
Thou art the Temple and the Deity of the Temple;
And thou art the worshipper !
The Beloved likes not the ventures of vanity,
And the Beloved cometh not home.
I fain would die a sacrifice at the feet of them that are
 informed of His Love !
I fain would be a slave of them that live inwardly in His
 hymn of Praise !
He loves the vestures dyed in Nam, in the madder dye
 of His Love,
When the dyer of Nam dyes the flesh-vestures of man,
 the colour is rich and pure,
The Brides whose garments are dyed gay rose of
 spiritual youth dwell in Him and He dwelleth in
 them !
I pray for the dust of the feet of the Brides !
He maketh, He decorateth and He dyeth The Bride with
 the colour of soul, Himself !
He cometh to love and taketh the Bride to His Bosom !
O Fond Bride ! Why art Thou seeking Him everywhere
 outside, when thy own heart is His Throne ?
In thy own heart, He waits for thee !

O Vain Girl-Bride !

Thy quivering limbs, thy restless feet cannot speed thee
  to Him !

They that have entered the God-lock Union say, that the
  way is through loving Him and not loving ourselves,
  to think as

He thinketh, to will as He willeth, to do what He
  willeth !

If the Bride loves and foregoes self,

If the Bride thinks of His lotus feet who bestoweth love !

If the Bride gives away all her mind and soul in love,

And counts no other day but that one day when He
  looks at her with His beaming smile,

And the Bride, dyed in bliss of love, stands straight,
  proud, unafraid, undisturbed, unmoved, preoccu-
  pied day and night as His wedded one,

And she lives in deep simplicity of her new home,
  Himself; no more restless, no more seeking rest,

Then and there is attained the perfection of beauty,
  wisdom, and love; she needs nothing else !

I sicken at pleasure, the pain heals me,

I may not forget Thee !

Thou the Creator of me ! What Thou doest is done, what
  I do is all an undoing !

Thou art the dweller in Thy Creation, further than
  furthest is Thy limit, and a still more art Thou !

Thou the magician livest in Thine own miracle;

The life burns in Thee, and Thou burnest in the flame
  of life,

And the living and the non-living art Thou;

None can breathe where Thou breathest and none know
  Thy thought.

All goes Thou makest it to go !

If palaces made of pearls, bedecked with rubies, stand
  before Thee;

If the walls and the floors are plastered with sandal,
  musk and agar—

Take not Thine eyes from the Vision of Reality !
Forget not, O Disciple, the Name of thy Beloved !
When taken away from my Beloved,
My soul takes fire and is burnt down !
If Thy whole estate be made of jewels and gems,
And thy halls are full of all means of pleasure,
And there wait upon thee silver-limbed damsels with
   their ruby lips whispering words of love to thee,
Take not thine eyes off the Vision of Reality !
Forget not, O Disciple, the Name of thy Beloved !
If all magical powers are thine,
And thou canst become invisible and visible at thy will,
And crowds worship thee,
Take not thine eyes off the Vision of Reality !
Forget not, O Disciple, the Name of thy Beloved !
Even if thou art a Sultan,
And thy cohorts await thy command,
It is all vanity !
Take not thy eyes off the Vision of Reality !
Forget not, O Disciple, the Name of thy Beloved !
O Jewel of my Heart !
I know no jeweller who could value Thee,
None who could teach me Thy worth !
Now Thou art mine !
All creations are in Thee !
And Thou art all creations' Self !
Enough, I see Thee a hundred times a day shining so
   rare in me !
Thou art the Seer of Thyself,
Thine own Price, Thine own Seller and Purchaser.
Yoked with this mind of mine, a wanderer and with this
   blood of ignorance so dense;
With these companions of mine, so blind and restless
   —how can I attain Thy goodness !
O Jewel of my heart ! Teach me Thine own rarity.
And let me touch my mind and heart with Thy gleams !
For I touch Thee, and I live;

I touch Thee again, and I live more.
They have read and read, and they have loaded the
    bullockcarts of knowledge—
They have loaded their camels and freighted their ships;
But where do they go ?
Only one thing counts, all else is froth and foam of an
    emptied self !
What is the meaning of being His servant if still the fear
    of Him remains ?
He is His servant who is not distinct from Him !

LOVE

I know not what they call Love, when they still can
    think of another and search for him !
They love who having seen Him see none else,
Who do not complain nor think of complaining.
The good, and bad, is merely how we take it;
They love not, who live in counting the favours and
    frowns of love.

(Guru Angad)

ALL IS WELL, IF I AM WITH HIM

He sows and He reaps, He makes and He keeps,
He sees His own glory; the raw and the ripe, all are His !
He who has come must also go.
Leave all things of man and nature and destiny alone !
Why should I forget my Beloved ?
I must make or mar myself with my own hands;
All is well if I am with Him !
If they bathe in a hundred waters, the dirt of sin-
    consciousness cannot be washed away thus : it
    remains;
But they have cast their dirt outside of themselves, who
    touch the silk of His Love within themselves !
They have realized the pure thought;

It is in the realization of their love that they laugh and
    weep;
They speak to us, or turn their backs, refusing to speak,
    as it pleaseth them
They reck of none and they heed nothing,
The rich majestic minds that think of Reality !

KARMA

All counting is for those who themselves count "me,
    thee—mine, thine"; and they must give full account
    of their own too.
His mill of judgement must roll and press oil as out of
    the oil-seeds !

WOMAN

Born of woman, nourished by woman, wedded to
    woman, why do they revile woman ?
Love is born in the heart of woman,
And the woman starts life ageing, and the race !
Why revile her that gives birth to kings amongst men,
The beauty is born of woman, there is no beauty
    without woman !
None can be without a woman !
Only that One alone is beyond sex,
Those lips are the Ruby of Fortune that open to name
    That Great One !
Afraid of Him the winds blow, blow, blow,
Afraid of Him the rivers flow, flow, flow !
The fire burns, and the earth lies firm and low !
Afraid of Him, the Indra, the king of nature, ordains,
Afraid of Him is the law of Justice.
Afraid of Him the suns and the moons run and run !
On the path of million miles unending, the orbs go, go,
    go !
In His awe the Heavens arch;

And all gods, all Buddhas and adepts speak and think !
The millions of creatures are running to and fro :
On the forehead of all is written their destined course !
Above all laws, above all destiny is He :
The Subject, the Absolute !

THE TEMPLE OF BREAD : LANGAR

What is a home, but a hospitable feasting of children
with bread and love and faith ? What is spiritual life in the
temple of flesh, without a full meal first ? The very first
Temple made by Guru Nanak, therefore, was the temple of
Bread, or Guru's Langar. In one common Temple of Bread,
the Bread of God was made free to the children of man. Let
none be hungry where the spirit of God prevails. The
Guru's people and the Guru were one home and one
family; but it was no Utopian idea, as of the democracy of
labour; it was the democracy of Soul, so gloriously invoked
in the temple of the human heart by the genius of the Guru.
The sacrifice of selfishness was made for the gladness of
soul that the act gave to the people, who came round Guru
Nanak. The soul of the people was so fully nourished and
satisfied that they could not entertain feelings of difference
and duality. We are not selfish when we are in the deep
repose of a dewy slumber. We are never selfish when we
are in love. The people came and laid their selfishness at his
feet, and begged a little of it for his service. To serve the
devotees was serving the Master. This union was so
spiritually cooperative that none knew if his own hands
were his own or of the devotees of the Guru. The bodies and
hearts and minds were mingling with each other and with
those of the Master, by the magic of His presence amongst
them. Here was a religion that made love and labour the
common property of man.

Today no Sikh with a grain of that faith in him can
possibly think that he owns the Bread. "Bread and water
belong to the Guru." No man who is initiated into the Path

of the Guru can own a home without being ready to share it with the Guru's people.

The fruits of his labour belong also to them. Such was the Master's foreshadowing of the future; and in this lay all the difference between him and the centuries of the purely Brahminical culture before him. "The people are more than myself," says the Guru. "Religion is inspiration of love. The Beloved is in His people and the service of God. And it is through service that love is realised. The spark of love is found by chance by some fortunate one in the company of His Saints and it is the reward of those who have surrendered themselves, head and heart, to the Divine."

The Master chose out his family of God's disciples; they served him and he served them. Real service of people is serving them with *life*, and the one who is *alive* can give *life* to others. So the Master says that the opportunity to serve God in humanity is His gift. They alone serve whom He gives the authority to do so.

Guru Nanak's passion for farming is a true index of his creative mind. We must labour to create the grain to feed people with. All other needs that we have are secondary; there is only one physical distress, and that is hunger. We all must labour on the land and sweat for our bread. Guru Nanak chose finally the life of a farmer for himself. The gardening and farming are outward symbols of the genius of art. We see in his disciples a rare combination of labour and spiritual vision of a home-life and a cave-life; not in a spirit of compromise, but in the spirit of that sweet reconciliation with which the flying bird flaps both his wings for his balance in the blue sky. Guru Nanak poured song into the heart of labour; and his greatest men were farmers, or the help mates of the farmers—such as masons who made huts, carpenters who made ploughs, smiths who made tools, and weavers who made garments for the saints. The entrance to this spiritual humanity lay through a small lowly door where selfishness could not pass. If the people could not drop their selfishness of their own accord, then the Guru's personality softly stole into theirs and helped them from within to drop it, without their knowledge.

Here do we find the Guru's inspiration of love achieving all that we still dream of but cannot accomplish. Our disease is not wars and crimes, and sins; but the selfishness of man, a disease more of the soul than of the flesh. Its cure lies in the direction in which worked Nanak, and not in any material readjustment. We need more men with their sensual nature cast out by the Grace of God, through His Favour.

It is remarkable that all the Nine Followers of Nanak kept his central idea of spiritual humanity—its formation, its love, and its service as the chief passion of their daily life, till this idea of his is seen emerging in perfect clearness in the time of Guru Gobind Singh, as Khalsa.

NANAK GIVES NEW MEANINGS TO OLD WORDS, AS DID BUDDHA

Lest his words "Guru", "Sant", "Dhyanam" etc., should be misunderstood in their old sense, he sings his now world-famous *Arti* to dispel all doubt as to his meaning. He sings of Him round whose Throne "wait a million prophets", "in the interval of Whose one eyewink there are a million creations that come and go !" Nanak's word, "Guru" does not mean a man; "Burnt be the tongue that calls him a man," says Arjun. "Hell is for those who call me God; I am His Slave !" says Gobind Singh. In vain is all imaging of man. "I do not know how to name Him. I only say 'Master, Guru, Hari Hari !' He is immeasureable, how can I measure Him." And no one else but Nanak is the Master, and he is the man.

"Guru Nanak" is a ten-fold, ten-figured personality, and the whole Sikh life as created and nurtured by the Ten Masters is the only key we have to the understanding of this word. Gobind Singh bluntly lays it down that the language of *Guru Granth* is to have no interpretation other than the life and art of Nanak himself. The interpreters of these teachings do not bridge the gulf that seems to lie between the language of Nanak and that of Gobind Singh; because they commit the mistake of not putting the Word of the Guru, or the Master, in its proper setting of Sikh life as manifested in His history, its birth and growth. The majesty of Guru Nanak's diction, the crystal clearness, the self-restraint, the composure, even in the flood of ecstasy, show the difference between him and the Bhaktas of mediaeval India with their confused clamour of Prakrit and Urdu.

We see Nanak's master-mind again when we find that he never preached, but only planted with his own hand the seedling of spiritual life in the soul of the disciple and watched it grow as a gardener watched plants. "The Guru put his hand on my forehead and made me an angel by his touch; all sin-consciousness was washed out of me and I now live in the beatific vision of the reality." The Guru sat in the heart of the disciple, consuming all sensual desire and leading the disciple, into perfect godhead. And when the disciple heard the voice of the Guru within himself, he caught it and went on, merely echoing and re-echoing the music of the Master's Nam.

The Hari Mandir itself is a glimpse into Sikh history. The Temple is a centre of perpetual worship, as a human heart, bathed in waters of peace, eternally isolated from the fires of desire that burn outside. The Sikh life must through luminous self-renunciation first bathe in the nectar and then enter within. After this glorious entrance, it is a life of continuous inspiration. In Sikh history, whenever the flames of outer fire leapt towards the Sikh, his Master quenched it in the surrounding nectar, and plunged the Sikh again into deep peace of the inner life.

GURU GOBIND SINGH

SELECTIONS AND FREE TRANSLATIONS FROM THE

DASAM GRANTHAM

I—FROM VACHITAR NATAK

I come down from the Hemkunta mountain of Seven
Horns of Snow, where I lay in sleep of power and
love in the Pure Being.

The Beloved has sent me down; and I come, my being
still pierced with the mystic light of His holy feet !

There is a pang of ecstasy in me, the pang of an ever-
awakened Vision of the Divine. I have seen Him, for
me the life is self-realized !

Do not call me God, I am His man come on earth to see
the Fire-works of His creation !

I think of Him who devours both Time and Space. He
is looking at me, and I do as His looks beckon me
to do.

I come singing His Nam, and I go sowing the seeds of
the Eternal.

II—FROM AKAL USTAT

I seek safety in Him !

I seek safety in Him, Who is the Steel of the Blood of
centuries !

I seek safety in Him, Who is the Heart of all ages !

I seek everlasting safety in Him, Who is the Iron of life.

I bow down to Him, Whose form is the Eternal Unity.

The One that meets us everywhere on land and in water !

The One dwelling above Time and Space, whose Aura is all the teeming life that is filling the fourteen Regions of the created worlds;

I bow down to the Divine Life that is manifest in the moving little ant and the elephant alike, and blesses the poor and the rich alike;

The Inscrutable One Who is the Knower in the life-throb of every heart;

The One that in Himself transcends all expression, and is undescribed by all descriptions.

I bow down to Him from whom the floods of life rolling come, and into whom all go and rest again;

Where the past, the present, and the future, are mere fiction.

And one little moment of devotion spent with Him is a whole Eternity.

I bow to Him Who is awakened Consciousness, and Who is the whole Unconscious Self that sleeps without waking;

Here He giveth without limit, and there He taketh away !

Here He putteth His hands out asking as a beggar for alms, and there He standeth at every door as the indefatigable Giver with His hands full to give away His all;

Here He follows the rulings of the Vedas, and there He disobeys them entirely; here He is the Infinite Appearance, and there He is All Silence—indistinguishable from Nothing; the Ever-Unknown, the Unknowable !

I bow to Him

Whom I see here as a warrior fully armed, and there a scholar seeking pure knowledge;

Who eats wind and fire here, Who is fettered in the love of woman there !

Who is the gods and the goddesses,

Who is both the Black and the White;

The Dweller in the fortress of *Dharma*, Who goes forth and is everywhere !

He is the Vow of celibacy, and He is the amorous Passion.

Nath (Lord) !

Thou art the Hindu, the Moslem, the Turk, and the Feringhi;

Thou art the Persian, the Sanskritan, the Arabian;

Thou art poet, the skilled dancer, the Songster Supreme.

Thou art the Speech; and Thou art the Avdhuta, the adept.

Thou art the Warrior clad in shining armour, and Thou art the Peace Supreme !

Thou art man, woman, child and God !

Thou art the Flute-player, the Herdsman that goes grazing His dumb cows !

Thou bestowest love, and Thou givest Thyself to all !

Thou art the protector of life and the giver of all prosperity !

Thou art the cure of all sorrows and suffering;

Thou art the net of the charms of youth, and high summit of all fulfilment !

Thou art the form of a beautiful Princess and Thou art the emaciated form of the *Brahmachari* with the wooden beads hanging from his neck;

Thou art the Muezzin that cries from the roof of the mosque, the Yogi that lies wrapt in silence of deep thought, unthinking in the soul-lit cave.

The Vedas art Thou, and the Quran !

In all shapes and everywhere, Thou art dear to me; in every form Thou art Thyself !

Thou art my Vow; my Dharma; my beginning, and end !

III—FROM JAP SAHIB : THE HYMN OF SALUTATIONS

I salute Him Whom none can name,
Whom none can enshrine in clay,
The Pure Being, the Spirit of Eternity,
The Beauty of life past all measures !
The Iridescent Soul : beyond all colour, and raiment,
    and caste, and race;
Whom even the gods name by not-naming, and so do
    the tiny blades of grass praise Him !
My salutations to Him, the Naked, through the colour
    and clothes of His Creation !
I salute Him whom no waters can ever wet,
Whom no sky doth cover;
The Ever-unstained by deeds and doings;
Who holds the orbs of heaven in His hands, and who
    Himself stands on nothing ?
In whom life touches no-life, science no-science; light
    and darkness are one, knowledge and ignorance both
    meet, pain and pleasure are not distinct, Dharma is
    Adharma, scriptures not-scriptures, and worlds no-
    worlds !
I salute Him,
The child in children,
The Orb in rolling orbs,
The Indra in Kings,
The beauty in kings, slaves and saints !
The great Fire, the great Seed, the great Unknown !
I bow to Him from Whom all things come,
In Whom all things are,
To Whom all things return,
The ancient Yogi, the Adept, the gem of charm !
I salute the Song,
The Skill of Perfection,
The Rhythm of Harmony of the Immeasurable—
Where the depths of rapturous Silence lie on the heights
    of holy chanting !
I salute the Stranger Whose eyes fascinate everyone !

The Figure of Renunciation, the Figure of Illumination !
The Man of Beauty, Joy, and Mystery,
The Ever-undescribed, the All-described,
With whose Names the pages of Creation are full.
I salute the Mother of Worlds,
I bow to the Knowledge Absolute;
The Kind One Who always thinks of us,
Who gives Love, light and life; and Who counts not !
The Speech of our speech, the Mind of our mind,
The soft, soft Light, the Ambrosia of Immortality !
Salutations to the Pure Being !
The Beginningless Beginning, the Infinite at all points;
The Self-absorbed, Unconscious-conscious, Avdhuta
    Supreme, that is seated everywhere as the Soul of all,
    deluging everything with His love !
Who overwhelms all living things with goodness,
The One, the Many, and the One again !
My Gobind, my Mukand, the Million-hearted, the
    Infinite Mind, my Hari, my Beloved !
The sea of million-waves, the One *Mai* unportioned by
    all-Difference.
The Beautiful Transience, and Transcendent Perma-
    nence !
The Sweet Sad One Who hath no cares !
Salutations to the Dharma, the light of goodness !
Salutations to the Beloved beyond all namings !
Salutations to the Splendour of Soul !
Salutations to the Kind One Who is always with us
Who is Glory Infinite, Glory ! Glory ! Everywhere.

IV—To His Disiciples

(Gathered from all over the Master's Writings)

Has the Truth I gave you yesterday lost its charm for
you ? Each one of you must find it for himself again. There
is nothing worth knowing but the Truth I have been telling
you ever since time began.

You have not understood the sweetest song; I have been singing to you in my last nine Incarnations. I did not mean that you should turn the only Truth of life again into a dead creed. I give you now these songs and leave you alone. These songs are my body and the living Temple of the Disciples. These hymns will be the Voice of the Guru to His Disciples. I name my successor when I name to you these Songs, as "Guru Granth."

I am the hearth-fire that gathers the night-bitten round its glow, and clothes the pilgrims of eternity with the mantle of flame. As they sit by me, I teach them the secrets of the hidden, life.

I am the light that cures blindness, I heal the wounds of darkness. I am the inspiration of Power. I make the sparrows of love destroy the eagles of hatred.

I lift my quiver off the shoulders of the sun, and I strike with my gold-tipped arrows the gloom of centuries.

I wrench my sword from the blue sky, and I utter my prayers as I smite the cords of ignorance that bind you.

When I see them leading helpless beings bound hand and foot to the place of execution to be slaughtered there to appease the ghosts of night, I rise and scatter the ghosts.

I carry the Hawk of White Plumage perched on my wrist, and in its claws is the bird of time.

I am the ever-lit Torch that goes on lighting the lamps of life,

I open new kingdoms for you; I start new dynasties for you, where there is no pain.

I am He whom you cannot forget. I come with a cleaving sword in my hand, and bring the day for you in its flash.

I am Truth, but bear no resemblance to descriptions they give of me to you in books.

I come. Truth is God, and we are of God; and the triumph is of Truth, and we are of Truth. If the mountains do not move aside, they will sink with grief; If the rivers do not part and give a passage, they will dry up, when I chant my Song of the Sword that God first flung into space out of Himself.

Do not come to me with offerings of flowers and sweets, bring me the blood of my ancestors. I will rise and offer myself to the people with a drawn sword in my hand.

Do they despise you ? Are you low caste ? I will enrobe you in a saffron-dyed garment of joy, and I will dissolve that Fire of Heaven in your blood before which the sun and moon melt in submission. You are the Chosen, the Divine Khalsa (the King's own).

Cobblers ! Tanners ! Weavers ! Washermen ! Brewers ! Heavy laden Labourers ! Farmers ! Come, take this Divine Light from my hands. It is for you, and you alone. It is the ancient Light of the Knowledge of God; Hold, it is your soul. Meditate on this supreme flame, and live in this day-glean; for this is Love. All else is illusion and death. The master song is life, His Nam is immortality. As long as it burns unflickering in you, you are the kings of righteous-ness—the Khalsa.

Man is one. God is one. Love is one. One with the inner Light, one with Truth, one with Love; live in the Silence and the Sound of Nam. You are the sons of the Khalsa.

All else is false and unsteady but that Light lit in your soul. He lives who loves; none else. Turn back within yourself; love the good, and hoard the abundance of Simran—thus shall you cut asunder the Noose of Yama, and win the Freedom of the Immortals.